Exploration
Journey through feelings, trust, and belief

Emotion Explosion • Trust Trek • Belief Blast-off

A Curriculum for Preteens

Exploration
Journey through feelings, trust, and belief

About the Authors

Churches, conventions, and seminars continue to seek *Linda Kondracki Sibley,* founder and executive director of Confident Kids, to train volunteers to minister to the needs of high-stress kids and families. Linda holds a master's degree in Christian education and pastoral care from Bethel Seminary and has fifteen years experience in church-related ministry to children and families. She is the author of the *Guides for Growing a Healthy Family* series published by Fleming H. Revell and a contributing editor for *Christian Parenting Today.*

Patricia Alderdice Senseman is a Christian educator. Formerly a director of children's ministries, she is a popular speaker at conventions and seminars. Patricia was an editor at Standard Publishing for seven years and continues to write and edit from her home in Cincinnati. She writes about trust from the trenches of her own relationships.

Jim Eichenberger brings two decades of Christian education experience to his writing. He has served as a teacher, principal, youth minister, freelance writer, editor, Christian school consultant, workshop speaker, and Sunday school teacher, among other roles. He currently leads the newly developed Christian school department at Standard Publishing Company.

Cover photo by Masterfile
Inside illustrations by Grannan Graphic Design
Computer designs by Peggy Theile

All Scripture quotations, unless otherwise indicated, are taken from the HOLY BIBLE NEW INTERNATIONAL VERSION®, NIV®. Copyright ©1973, 1978, 1984 by International Bible Society. Used by permission of Zondervan Publishing House. All rights reserved.

The Standard Publishing Company, Cincinnati, Ohio. A Division of Standex International Corporation. ©1997 The Standard Publishing Company
All rights reserved. Printed in the United States of America

03 02 01 00 99 98 97 96   5 4 3 2 1
ISBN 0-7847-0646-8

Exploration
Journey through feelings, trust, and belief

Beyond childhood, heading to the next level, preteens seek to discover the importance of realities they cannot see. Help them sort out their feelings, grasp the concept of trust, and act on their beliefs. Help them learn the secrets to winning in real life!

Unit 1 — Emotion Explosion — 9

Written by Linda Kondracki Sibley to help kids develop the ability to name their feelings and express them appropriately.

Session 1	Your Feelings—A Gift From God	15
Session 2	Permission to Speak Appropriately, Captain!	23
Session 3	Who's in Control Here?	29
Session 4	Danger Ahead!	36
Bridge the Gap	Family Feelings	43
Go to Extremes	I Feel for You!	48

Unit 2 — Trust Trek — 52

Written by Patricia Alderdice Senseman to help kids understand and build trusting relationships with kids, adults, and especially God. Emphasize prayer.

Session 1	Blast Off!	56
Session 2	Trusting Comrades	63
Session 3	You're Breaking Up . . .	69
Session 4	Trust Trek With God	76
Bridge the Gap	Trust Trek Trip	83
Go to Extremes	A Prayer Walk	87

Unit 3 — Belief Blast-off — 90

Written by Jim Eichenberger to help kids clarify a belief system and develop a basic Christian theology.

Session 1	God—In Charge at Mission Control	94
Session 2	Man—Lost in Space	100
Session 3	Jesus—Sent on the Universe's Greatest Rescue Mission	106
Session 4	Other Christians—Flying in Differing Spacecraft	111
Bridge the Gap	Faith Fleet Academy	119
Go to Extremes	Creating the Captain's Log	123

Why "Next Level"?

Upper elementary kids—we'll call them preteens—are reaching, striving, groping toward the next level. They're in transition. They want to be taller, stronger, faster, and smarter—as they catapult on their way to the next level.

In some ways preteens appear already to have arrived at the next level, (once termed junior high). Preteens want to wear the right clothes, match hairstyles with athletes or rock stars, and fit in with the peer group no matter what! For many, however, the next level is an elusive goal: manly muscles and feminine curves are controlled by hormones not purchasing power.

So, too, the limits on thought structure. Many, if not most, fifth and sixth graders lack the ability to think critically, to form logical arguments, or draw general principles from specific examples. There is usually a wide gulf between their level of experience and their ability to reflect on the meaning of their experiences.

Preteens are also still resolving the issue: *What can I do well?* rather than tackling the adolescent question: *Who am I?* So when preteens dress and act like their peers they are striving for self-acceptance—feeling that they are as up-to-date as their peers, rather than establishing a personal identity. Erickson's studies show that ten to twelve year olds are less involved with establishing a personal identity than they are with figuring out what they're really good at. This disparity creates difficulties for those using junior high curriculum for preteen classes: What you see (a teenager) is not what you get (concrete-operational thinking and a different life task).

Next Level curriculum is transitional: to help transitional preteens feel comfortable in teen-style learning settings and to equip leaders to teach within the limits of preteen development. Lessons are structured to help you teach preteens effectively in groups. The younger the student, the more discussion guidance must be given to identify appropriate conclusions, and to suggest appropriate actions to be taken.

While many junior high topics are helpful and many elective curriculums look age appropriate, they often do not work with preteens because they were not designed for preteens' limited thought processing and inexperienced discussion skills.

Next Level Preteen Electives! Planned and designed with preteen issues in mind and tailored for the learning capabilities of concrete thinkers! Visually appealing for the video generation. Emotionally satisfying for techno-driven kids.

This curriculum offers bonus opportunities for preteens to **Go to Extremes** serving others. It also strives to build family relationships—**Bridge the Gap**—during fun-filled family session.

So, because life is not a game—
pick a topic and recruit some helpers.
Start a group for ten to twelve year olds—
They'll be glad you did!

Next Level Preteen Electives address the importance of instilling values for character development.

You can use **Next Level Preteen Electives** confidently, knowing that they are based on core biblical principles, permeated with Bible teaching, and presented in a way that ten to twelve year olds can understand and enjoy!

How are Next Level units organized?

Get Into the Game

As an introduction to the session, this section offers activities to grab the students' attention and encourages participation from the entire group.

These lesson steps offer activity choices that may be set up as learning centers or used as options. Depending on the class size, the teacher may divide the class into smaller groups to complete the activity. Each group works on the activity. For this to be effective, the teacher needs ample assistance.

If the class is small, the teacher can customize the session accordingly. Select one or two options to use or have the class work together instead of dividing into small groups.

Step 1

This activity is designed to help students dig deeper into the topic. This section always includes a biblical study.

Step 2

This section offers another way to discover biblical truth.

Step 3

This activity involves the entire class to help students apply what they learned in Steps 1 and 2.

Take It to the Next Level

This final section concludes the session by helping students commit the principles they have learned to their own lives. The question, "So what does this mean to me personally?" can be answered in this section.

Extra Helps

Each unit introduction includes devotion suggestions for the teacher and/or the students. The devotional ideas correlate with the sessions contained in that unit.

Reproducible pages are provided for your convenience. Photocopy these pages for your use or for your students' use to enhance each session.

Additional Resources

The following list of books and music serve as extra resources for each unit. Feel free to use these materials as research for teaching or as extra activities.

Unit 1—Emotion Explosion

All My Feelings Are Okay by Linda Kondracki. Published by Revell Publishers
Good Grief by Granger Westberg, Augsburg Fortress
"How Are You Feeling Today" posters. These posters contain thirty cartoon-style faces expressing different emotions. The posters can help kids name their feelings accurately. The posters come in 8 1/2" x 11" or a 24" x 36" classroom wall size. You can order these items from Confident Kids Support Groups, 330 Stanton Street, Arroyo Grande, CA 93420, FAX (805) 473-7948.
"Cry Me to Sleep" by Spooky Tuesday (Innocent Media)
"Song for Paul" by 100 Days (Liquid Disc)

Unit 2—Trust Trek

When God Doesn't Make Sense by James Dobson, Tyndale
"Father, Thy Will Be Done" and "There You Are" by Carolyn Arends (Reunion)
"My Trust Is In the Name of the Lord" by Laurie Jasurda (Integrity's Hosanna! Music)
"Will Trust" by Erin O'Donnell (Cadence)

Unit 3—Belief Blast-off

13 Lessons in Christian Theology by Denver Sizemore, College Press
Basic Christianity by John R. W. Stott, Eerdmans
Charts of Christian Theology by Wayne H. House, Zondervan
Concise Theology by J. I. Packer, Tyndale House Publishers
Know What You Believe by Paul E. Little, SP Publications
(See the unit introduction, page 92, for music suggestions.)

A Ministry of Confident Kids

If the preteens in your group would benefit from more focused help on the issue of decision making, Standard Publishing offers a distinctively Christian support-group curriculum.

Facing My Feelings
Living in My Family
Making Wise Choices
Growing Through Changes

provides help for hurting kids and struggling parents. Written by Linda Kondracki Sibley, the curriculum guide includes support-group session plans for preschool through preteen, plus a parent guide as well. Information for program administrators—complete with reproducible forms—is provided.

FACING MY FEELINGS helps kids and parents understand that:
- All our feelings are OK.
- There are healthy ways to talk about and deal with our feelings.
- We have a feeling vocabulary and ways to label what we are feeling.
- Our feelings tell us when we need to ask for help.
- Jesus understands us, and His presence with us is the greatest source of help we have for facing our feelings.

LIVING IN MY FAMILY helps kids and parents understand that:
- Every family is special and unique.
- There are no perfect families.
- Changes in family life disrupt our sense of security but we can adapt.
- Coping skills help us when our family doesn't or can't meet our needs.
- We need to develop basic skills to communicate in our family.
- Belonging to God's family gives us strength and security.

MAKING WISE CHOICES helps kids and parents understand that:
- We always have choices, no matter what the situation.
- There's a process we can follow to make wise choices.
- God's Spirit with us is our most valuable resource for choosing wisely.
- We can identify wise people who can help us make intelligent choices.

GROWING THROUGH CHANGES helps kids and parents understand that:
- Change is a natural part of God's design for our world.
- There are healthy ways to respond to change.
- Changed circumstances always pass and hurts heal.
- God is a constant friend and guide through every change.

Unit 1

Emotion Explosion

Feelings—we all have them. They are part of the human experience. Throughout our lifetimes, we all experience a wide spectrum of feelings: from the heights of ecstasy to the pits of depression; from deep love to deep hatred; from empowering self-confidence to crippling shame. On some days, feelings can seem like a wonderful blessing from God, while on other days we think they are God's curse! That is the nature of feelings. They move us up and down through the human experience. Yet, would any of us want a life without them? Can we begin to imagine a life without love or joy or peace or self-fulfillment? "No," we may reply, "but I can well imagine a life without anger or hatred or bitterness!" Therein lies the great paradox about feelings: We cannot have it both ways! We cannot fully experience love without knowing hatred; we cannot embrace joy without first knowing despair; and true peace comes only to those who have survived the great storms of life!

So why do many in our society have such a difficult time managing the emotional side of life? Perhaps because early in life we discover that many of the feelings in the human experience are not much fun to feel, and we begin to find ways to avoid feeling them. But, try as we might, we cannot control our feelings by wishing them away, pretending they don't matter, or trying to cover them up with drugs, alcohol, or food. Unless we can come to terms with the immutable truth that the only

Session 1
Guideline for Managing Feelings: All of my feelings are valuable gifts from God.
Know that all feelings are a gift from God.
Feel accepting of all their feelings, especially the difficult ones.
Use a prayer journal to express their feelings to God.

Session 2
Guideline for Managing Feelings: All my feelings need to be expressed in healthy and appropriate ways.
Know the dangers of stuffing their feelings.
Feel equipped to express their feelings in ways appropriate to their personalities.
Use prayer as a means of expressing their feelings to God.

Session 3
Guideline for Managing Feelings: I can be in control of my feelings rather than letting my feelings be in control of me!
Know four keys to staying in control of their feelings.
Feel empowered to handle confusing and overwhelming feelings.
Trust God to help them stay in control of their emotions.

Session 4
Guideline for Managing Feelings: With God's Spirit in my heart, rage, bitterness, jealousy, and envy won't have a chance to start!
Know that rage, bitterness, jealousy, and envy are strong feelings that can easily lead to destructive actions.
Feel alert and prepared to handle different feelings when they arise.
Use prayer as a defense against rage, bitterness, jealousy, and envy.

way to manage our feelings is to *feel them,* we can never live a healthy and fulfilling emotional life as God intended!

For the next few weeks, you will have the opportunity to address this subject with your preteens and to teach them some important skills for managing their feelings according to the guidelines God has given us in His Word. This is a powerful unit for preteens who are entering puberty—a particularly vulnerable time for them emotionally. In the months and years ahead, they will experience more ups and downs in their feelings than at any other time of their lives. Without a proper understanding of the role feelings play in their lives and skills to handle them appropriately, preteens may let their feelings take control and lead them into unhealthy and destructive behaviors. This unit will prepare your kids to understand and handle their feelings as God intended, to help them live a more enjoyable and safe life.

As you prepare to teach this unit, familiarize yourself with the following key concepts.

1. Feelings are not good or bad. The first mistake we make concerning our emotional lives is to label the feelings we like to feel as good and the ones we don't like to feel as bad. By labeling them in this way, we set ourselves up to try to rid ourselves of feelings such as anger, fear, and guilt. Your preteens need to know that all their feelings are created by God, including the ones they don't like to feel. You will have an opportunity to teach them that. Rather than rid themselves of unpleasant feelings, they can learn to pay attention to the valuable messages their feelings give them.

2. Feelings will be expressed—in one way or another. Sometimes our feelings can seem so overwhelming we try not to deal with them at all. We think that if we ignore them or stuff them inside they will go away. But feelings cannot be handled in this way. Your preteens will learn that all their feelings will be expressed in one way or another. If they do not make wise choices to handle their feelings as they arise, the feelings will eventually build and cause all kinds of problems, such as making kids sick or leading them into unwise, unhealthy behaviors.

3. Naming feelings accurately is vital to managing them in healthy ways. One of the goals of this unit is to help your preteens build a feelings word vocabulary. Your preteens will learn that the first step in managing their feelings is to be able to name them accurately. They will see how naming their feelings frees them to make wise choices about how to deal with them. For instance, if we know we feel lonely, we can do something, such as call a friend, to relieve our loneliness. But if we can only say, "I feel bad," we cannot make a wise choice because we have not isolated, or named, what the real problem is.

Page 14 contains an alphabetical list of feeling words. This is by no means an exhaustive list, but you will use it throughout the unit to help your kids increase their awareness of the many feelings God has placed within them.

4. If we do not control our feelings, our feelings will control us. During puberty, your preteens' feelings will often seem so overwhelming and confusing, they won't know what to do. During these times, they are in the greatest danger of letting feelings control their common sense. This almost always leads to impulsive, destructive behaviors. You will help them learn steps to take to stay in control of their feelings, no matter how confusing or overwhelming the feelings may seem.

5. Since God has created all of our feelings, He can give us the power to use them as they were meant to be used. Throughout this unit, you will guide your preteens to draw on God's great power to help them control and use their emotional lives as God intended—to live a happier and safer life. Each week, kids will use both a prayer journal and a guided prayer activity to help them honestly express their feelings to God and to ask His Spirit to help them make wise choices.

Session Summaries/Features

Session 1. In this first session, your preteens will discover that God created all their feelings to help them live healthier and safer lives. They will explore how feelings such as anger, fear, loneliness, and sadness are important to their lives.

Session 2. Many kids learn early in life to bury the feelings they don't like to feel by choosing not to feel them (known as stuffing our feelings). This session will help preteens discover that stuffing their feelings is not an effective way to manage them. The preteens will explore methods for expressing their feelings in healthy and appropriate ways. They will also learn to recognize and avoid inappropriate ways of expressing their feelings.

Session 3. This session will teach four keys to help preteens stay in control when their feelings seem confusing and overwhelming. They will learn that controlling their feelings, instead of letting their feelings control them, happens when they do the following: 1. Think before acting; 2. Accurately name what they are feeling; 3. Make a wise choice about the feeling(s) and trust God to help.

Session 4. Although all of our feelings are OK, certain feelings tend to lead to an explosion of inappropriate and destructive behaviors. We can get hurt by feelings such as rage, bitterness, jealousy, and envy if we don't approach them carefully. In this session, preteens will learn the emotional signals to look for and strategies for staying out of the danger zone when facing potentially destructive feelings.

Bridge the Gap. This session will help families explore the subject of managing feelings in their homes. They will work together to identify words and actions that bring pleasant feelings to their family lives, as well as the words and actions that spur family upheaval. All families will leave this session committed to one new strategy for positively managing feelings within their homes.

Go to Extremes. This session will help kids develop empathy by learning to pay attention to what others are feeling. They will learn about kids in the world, and in their communities, whose life circumstances make it difficult to live happy lives. They can then participate in a service project to offer caring, loving support to some of these kids.

Prayer Journals. Throughout this unit, you will emphasize the importance of expressing our feelings to God in prayer, and you will teach the kids how to use a prayer journal. The prayer journals created in **Session 1** will be used each week, so make extra copies for kids who are not regular attendees and those who forget to bring their journals to class. Encourage the kids to use their journals by keeping one yourself and sharing a page from it each week. You can also offer small rewards to those who use their journals at home and bring them each week.

Scripture/Devotionals

To prepare for this unit, reflect on the following Scriptures as they relate to accepting and expressing God's gift of feelings in your life.

Philippians 4:6, 7—We don't have to anxiously avoid anything we are feeling, but can express all of our feelings honestly to God, asking Him for what we need. When we trust God to help us, His peace replaces our turmoil. Write a prayer expressing your most anxious feelings to God, asking Him for what you need, and giving thanks for what He will do for you. Look for His peace as you begin to rest in His presence and care.

Psalm 51:6—God desires truth in our inward parts. When we stuff our feelings, we are *not* being truthful. With God's help, we can honestly and openly face even difficult or scary feelings. In prayer this week, ask God to help you honestly embrace and express to Him your most private and scary feelings. Name them specifically and claim God's power to help you deal with them. Look for their power over you to disappear as you name them and invite God to be present in the midst of them.

Jonah 1:1-17 and 4:1; Matthew 27:1-5; Matthew 4:1-11; 1 Samuel 1:1-18—Read about these people in the Bible who struggled with powerful feelings. Two expressed them in ways that let their feelings take control of them; the other two took control of their feelings. What principles for maintaining control of your feelings, rather than letting your feelings control you, can you learn from these people's lives?

Ephesians 4:26; Galatians 5:22—Powerful feelings such as anger, bitterness, and envy cannot become destructive in your life when God's Spirit grows His Fruit in you. Focus on one specific fruit of the Spirit that would be the antidote to your most powerful and frightening feeling, and ask God to grow that fruit in you this week.

Alphabetical List of Feeling Words

accepted
afraid
angry
anxious
anxious to please others
apathetic
appreciated
ashamed
awkward

beaten
beautiful
bewildered
bitter
brave

calm
cheated
closed
comfortable
compassionate
competent
concerned
confident
confused
contented
cowardly
cruel
curious
cut off

dangerous
defeated
depressed
deprived
deserving punishment
desperate
disappointed in myself
disappointed in others

disgusted
dominated

eager
embarrassed
envious
excited
exhausted

fat
failure, like a
faithful
fearful
friendly
friendless
frustrated

gentle
grateful
grudge-bearing
guilty
gutless

happy
hated
hateful
hopeful
hopeless
hostile
hurt

ignored
impatient
inadequate
incompetent
in control
indecisive
insecure
inhibited
insincere
inferior
isolated

jealous
judgmental

kind

lonely
loser, like a
loved
loyal

manipulated
manipulative
melancholy
misunderstood

needy
nerdy

optimistic
off the wall
out of control
over-controlled
overlooked

paranoid
patient
peaceful
persecuted
pessimistic
phony
pleased
possessive
pouty
pressured
proud

quiet

rageful
rejected
repulsive
restrained
real

sad
secure
shy
sick
silly
sincere
sinful
sluggish
soft
sorry
stubborn
stupid
sunshiny
superior
supported
suspicious
sympathetic

terrified
threatened
tired
torn
touchy

ugly
unable to communicate
unappreciated
uncertain
understanding
up-tight
useless

victimized
vengeful
violent

weepy
weary
winner, like a
wishy-washy

zealous

Session 1

Your Feelings— A Gift From God

Scripture: Various selections illustrating the wide range of feelings God has given us
Key Verse: Philippians 4:6, 7

Guideline for Managing Feelings: All of my feelings are valuable gifts from God.
Know that all feelings are a gift from God.
Feel accepting of all their feelings, especially the difficult ones.
Use a prayer journal to express their feelings to God.

Get Into the Game

As students arrive, direct them to a table that has been covered with butcher or shelf paper. Supply magazines and newspapers with pictures of people showing various emotions. Instruct kids to cut out and paste the pictures of as many different feelings as they can find. When the paper is full, have them use felt tip markers to write the names of the feelings being expressed in large letters across the pictures. Display the completed collage on a wall or bulletin board.

Then say, "You may have guessed that we are going to spend the next few weeks talking about feelings. God has created each one of us with the ability to feel many different feelings, and each one is important to our lives. What are some of the feelings you listed on your collage?" Allow time for response. "As we continue this study, you will see that even feelings such as anger and sadness play an important role in our lives!"

Materials
magazines, newspapers, butcher or shelf paper, glue or paste, scissors, felt tip markers, tape

Step 1

Before the session, write the following Scripture references on index cards or slips of paper. Then hide the Scriptures around the room and, if possible, outside. Give the students five to ten minutes to find the cards. When they are finished, have them find the references in their Bibles, take turns reading the verses aloud, and name the feeling expressed in each. Ask kids to write that feeling next to the reference and place the cards or slips in the middle of the table. Also, write the names of the feelings on the chalkboard or a flip chart the kids can see easily throughout this activity.

Materials
Bibles, index cards or slips of paper, pens or pencils, chalk and chalkboard or a flip chart and marker

Joshua 1:9—terrified, courageous, discouraged
Job 19:14—abandonment
Job 19:7—wronged; falsely accused
Psalm 66:1, 2—joy, praise
Psalm 66:16—grateful
Psalm 22:1—abandoned, forsaken
Psalm 22:19-21—helpless, powerless
Psalm 23:4—safe, confident, trusting
Psalm 91:5—trust, fear
Psalm 51:1—guilty
Psalm 51:7, 10—forgiven
Matthew 6:31—worry
Matthew 21:12, 13—anger
John 11:32-36—sadness, grief
John 3:16—love
Acts 5:1, 2—greed
Ephesians 4:31—bitterness, rage
Ephesians 4:32—compassion, kind
Philippians 4:6—anxious

Say, "Believe it or not, this is not a complete list of all the feelings God has given us. We experience many other feelings in our lives." Divide kids into pairs and give them two or three minutes to write down as many feeling words as they can think of that are *not* on the list. Then have kids read their words to each other and eliminate any duplicates. Add slips with the new feeling words to the pile in the middle of your table. Now have the students work together to sort all the cards into two piles: those they consider to be "good" feelings and those they would classify as "bad" feelings. Refer to the piles and ask, "What is the difference between a good feeling and a bad feeling?" (Allow time for response. We usually label those feelings we don't like to experience as bad.) "You may not realize it, but there is no such thing as a bad feeling! Some feelings are not pleasant or fun to feel, but they are still important to our lives. We can say that there are *pleasant* and *difficult* feelings rather than good or bad feelings because all our feelings are important!" Place all cards or slips into a bag to be used later in the session.

Step 2

Say, "Feelings are important to God; He gave each one to us for a reason. Our feelings do many things for us. Without pleasant feelings we could never experience all the best things in life such as being loved and loving others or enjoying parties, carnivals, and roller coasters. Without difficult feelings we could not stay safe. We would never know when we were in danger,

Materials
poster board with the title "Important Guidelines for Managing My Feelings"

had lost something important to us, needed to say 'I'm sorry' or needed to make some new friends." Review the following feelings with the kids, guiding them to verbalize what each does for them:

1. fear—a warning that we are in danger.

2. anger—a warning that something wrong has happened (or at least we think something wrong has happened) to us that we need to do something about; it is also a warning that we could do something destructive.

3. love—tells us our need for relationships is being met properly.

4. lonely—is a signal that our need for relationships isn't being met properly.

5. sad—tells us we have been hurt in some way and need to take care of ourselves.

6. proud—tells us we have done something well.

7. guilty—tells us we have done something wrong that we need to make right.

8. excited—tells us something good is happening or is about to happen.

Say, "All these things are part of how God created us and what makes us human. But that's not to say that handling all these feelings is easy! It can be very hard because when we experience feelings we don't want to feel, our first response is to do hurtful things to ourselves or others to make the feelings go away. That is where we can get into trouble. So in the next few weeks, we will learn how to be aware of all our feelings and respond to them in ways that help us grow, not get us into trouble! We will learn some important guidelines for managing our feelings so they don't manage us! The first guideline is this: Recognize that all your feelings, even the difficult ones, are valuable gifts from God to help you live a safe and enjoyable life."

Display a poster containing the title, "Important Guidelines for Managing My Feelings" and write this first guideline on it: All my feelings are valuable gifts from God. Say, "When we realize that all our feelings—even the difficult ones—are gifts that help us, we have taken the first step to using our feelings the way God intended."

Step 3

Say, "Because our feelings are gifts from God, we need to get to know all of them. What do we do when we're trying to get to know someone?" (*Find out their names and some things about them.*) "It's the same with our feelings; the first step to knowing them is knowing their names." Divide the class into

Materials
true and false signs

groups of two or three and have each group draw a slip out of the bag from Step 1. Give them time to devise a short skit that will act out their feeling word to the rest of the class. Tell them they can use dialogue, but they cannot say the feeling word at any time. When all are ready, have the groups present their skits while the rest of the class tries to guess what feeling is being portrayed.

When all the skits have been presented and the feelings identified say, "Naming our feelings is the first step in knowing them, but we also have to know something about them."

Display two signs in different parts of your room—one that says *True* and the other *False.* Read the first statement from the list below. Ask kids to stand under the sign that depicts whether they think the statement is true or false. When all have made their selections, ask them to explain their choices. Then repeat the process, using the rest of the statements. Have kids sit down and go over each one, giving the correct answers:

1. It's OK for girls to be emotional, but boys need to be tough. *(False—God gave boys as many emotions as girls.)*

2. Everyone experiences emotional ups and downs. *(True—no one is happy all the time.)*

3. A person should never be angry. *(False—anger is an emotion like any other. We do, however, need to be very careful how we express our anger.)*

4. Crying is good for your health. *(True—crying releases tension and has a calming effect.)*

5. If you have painful feelings, you have done something wrong. *(Although in some instances our actions can produce painful feelings as a general rule this is false—hurtful things happen to us all of our lives.)*

6. There is no such thing as a bad feeling. *(By now, hopefully all your students will know this is true.)*

Take It to the Next Level

Say, "Since God has given us our feelings, He delights in having us talk to Him about them. David is an excellent model for this. He wrote the Psalms as prayers and songs to express his feelings to God. We looked at some of these earlier and saw many feelings David poured out to God. Did you know that David's Psalms talk about almost every kind of feeling? David told God when he was feeling happy and thankful for all the things God did for him; he told God when he was angry because God didn't do something David expected him to do; and he poured out his hurt feelings when friends betrayed or abandoned him. In fact, David's Psalms are so important,

Materials
poster of Philippians 4:6, 7, photocopies of prayer journal cover on page 21, photocopies of page 22 (copy on both sides and make five copies per student), stapler, small notebook to track kids' prayer requests

people have used them as prayers and songs to help them express their feelings to God for thousands of years!

"Although David wrote his Psalms thousands of years ago, the experience of writing our feelings to God in the form of prayers, poetry, or music is still one of the most important ways we have to manage our feelings today." Distribute photocopies of the cover and five inside pages (front and back) of "My Book of Psalms" prayer journals on pages 21 and 22. Have kids assemble them by stapling the cover to the inside pages. Display a poster of Philippians 4:6, 7 and have the class say it with you. Point out that this verse is a good summary of what happens when we pray honestly to God about our feelings. Presenting our requests and trusting God to answer them reduces our anxiety and helps us find His peace. Read the verses together several times.

Now guide kids to fill out the first page of their journals, reminding them that they are actually creating a psalm to the Lord. Go over each section, sharing the following information about each. (Note: You can help your students understand how to fill out their prayer journal pages by showing them a page you have filled out for yourself.)

1. Sections 1 and 2. The purpose of the first two sections is to help kids focus their thoughts and feelings. The first list reflects subjects found in the Psalms. In addition to thanking and praising the Lord, David often expressed his feelings over events that happened to him or things he had done, injustices he experienced or saw, or asked God his soul searching questions. Have kids check one subject they want to talk to God about today, and then choose the feeling word that most closely describes how they are feeling about it.

2. Prayer to the Lord. Next, they can express their thoughts and feelings as a prayer. Assure them this is a private prayer in which they are to honestly express themselves, rather than writing what they think they should say.

3. PS. Finally, this is an affirmation that no matter what happens in our lives or what we are feeling, God never stops loving or caring for us. This is also an element from David's Psalms. Even in those containing his most difficult feelings, David closes with an affirmation of accepting God's presence in his life.

End your session by having kids share key prayer requests with each other. Write these down in a small notebook that you can use each week to track kids' requests and pray for them at home. Have a prayer time together, beginning with a few moments of silent prayer during which kids can talk with God about whatever they may be feeling today. Close with a prayer for all your students.

Before they leave, encourage kids to fill out several pages in their journals this week. Offer a small incentive to those who bring their journals back with completed pages (see Unit Introduction for more information on using the prayer journals throughout the unit).

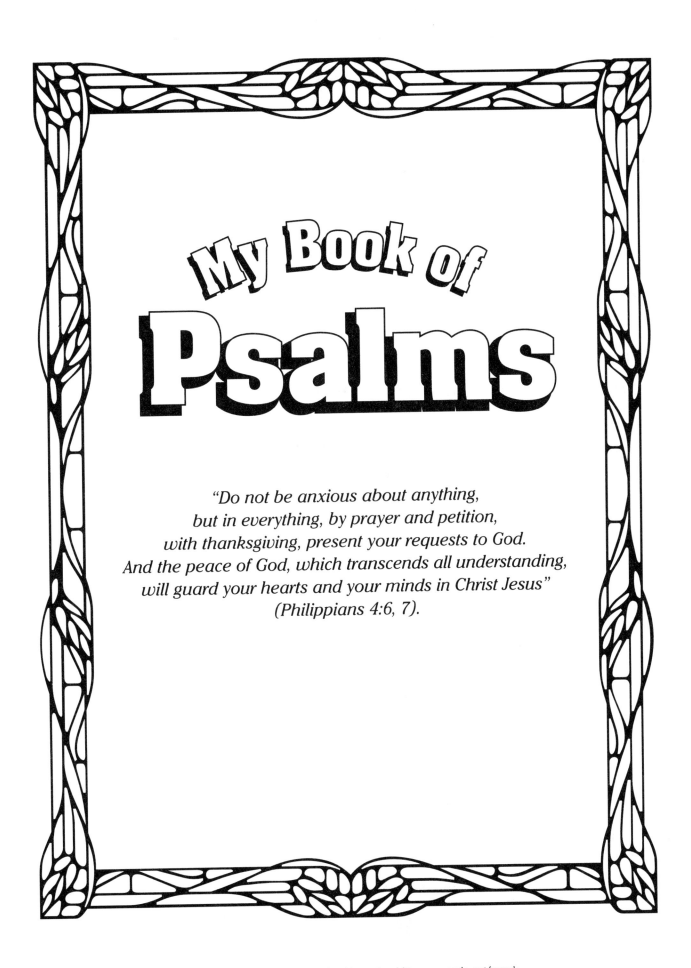

My Book of Psalms

Date: _____

Today I want to talk to God about:

_____ Something that happened: _____
_____ Something I did: _____
_____ A question I have: _____
_____ A complaint I have: _____
_____ Something I am thankful for: _____

I'm feeling (circle one):

Happy • Sad • Mad • Guilty • Afraid

Loving/loved • Proud • Other: _____

Dear God,

_____
_____
_____
_____
_____
_____
_____
_____

P.S. Thank you that no matter what I feel today, you love me and I can trust you to work everything out according to your plan for my life.

Session 2

Permission to Speak Appropriately, Captain!

Scripture: Galatians 6:2; Ephesians 4:26; 29-32; Philippians 4:6
Key Verse: Psalm 51:6

Guideline for Managing Feelings: All my feelings need to be expressed in healthy and appropriate ways.
Know the dangers of stuffing their feelings.
Feel equipped to express their feelings in ways appropriate to their personalities.
Use prayer as a means of expressing their feelings to God.

Get Into the Game

As students arrive, direct them to a table containing modeling clay, a plastic cup, liquid detergent, baking soda, and vinegar. Working in pairs, have kids form a cone-shaped volcano around the cup. Then have them place 1/8 cup of baking soda and 1/4 cup of liquid detergent into their cones. Next, have them add 1/3 cup of vinegar and enjoy watching their volcanoes become active! Tell the students that you will be using this volcano again later in the session. (Note: You may want to premeasure the ingredients before the session.)

Materials
modeling clay, liquid detergent, baking soda, vinegar, measuring cup, small plastic cup (large enough to hold one cup of liquid)

Step 1

Before the session, select four players for the skits and give them photocopies of the scripts so they can prepare. (You could allow the same student to portray Sara in both skits.) Have them present the skits. Afterwards ask, "Why do you think Sara responded to Jackie's news the way she did?" *(She was hurt, but didn't want to feel it.)* "What do you think made her explode at her mom when she didn't care all that much about the TV program?" *(Her stuffed feelings about Jackie's move finally came out.)*

Say, "One of the hardest parts of managing our feelings is knowing what to do with the feelings we don't want to feel. Everyone has trouble dealing with feelings such as anger, sadness, loneliness, or fear. Most of us try everything we can to avoid feeling them. Like Sara, we hope that ignoring the painful feelings will make them go away. We call this stuffing our feelings. Unfortunately, stuffing our feelings never makes them go away. The stuffed feelings just collect inside us.

Materials
photocopies of pages 27 and 28, Bibles, chalk and chalkboard or flip chart and marker

Speak Appropriately

Here is an important rule about managing our feelings—they must be expressed before they will go away. If we don't express them, they will eventually come out all by themselves, usually in a way we do not want them to! That's what happened to Sara. When her feelings caught up with her, it just took one little thing (not being able to see a favorite TV show) to set off her feelings. Now she is upset, her Mom is upset, and neither of them know exactly what's wrong.

"Sara could have avoided all that if she had known about today's guideline for managing feelings, which is to remember that *all* our feelings need to be expressed in healthy and appropriate ways. Today we will find out what that means. Since God gave us all our feelings, He also gave us some great rules for expressing them, so let's start with looking in the Bible."

Distribute slips of paper with the following references written on them so each class member has one verse, repeating references as necessary. Allow a few minutes for all to read their verses silently and think about what the verse says. Next, group all those with the same verse and let them come up with a rule for expressing feelings from the verse. Ask each group to read their verse to the rest of the class and share the rule. Write these rules on the board or a flip chart.

1. Ephesians 4:26—When you are angry, don't do anything destructive (sinful).

2. Galatians 6:2—Talk about your difficult feelings with others (carry each others burdens).

3. Philippians 4:6—Express your feelings to God in prayer and ask Him for help; thank Him when He answers.

4. Ephesians 4:29-31—Don't express your feelings with destructive words or actions.

5. Ephesians 4:32—Use kindness and forgiveness to express your feelings.

Summarize these rules by saying, "You can express your feelings to others and God in any way that is not hurtful or destructive to yourself, to others, or to property." Write this summary statement on the board or flip chart.

Step 2

Use the volcano from the Get Into the Game section, but use paint or a sharp instrument to add detail to make it look like a person's body. Place the baking soda and liquid detergent inside and the small styrofoam ball on top to make the head. Then have a student read Psalm 51:6. Say, "One of the things God means when He asks us to have truth in the inward parts is that he wants us to be honest about our feelings. When we stuff our feelings, we are not being truthful in our inner parts.

Materials

small styrofoam ball, paint and paintbrush or butter knife, 1/8 cup of baking soda, 1/4 cup of liquid detergent, 1/3 cup of vinegar, large box containing a prayer journal, pillow, box of tissues, running shoes, writing paper and pens, drawing paper and markers, a telephone directory, and a large red heart, poster board with feeling guideline from last session

As we said earlier, stuffing our feelings does not make them go away. It is only a form of lying to ourselves. And because the feelings are still there, they will eventually find a way out. When they do, it will usually be in a way that is worse than if we chose to express them ourselves."

Pour the vinegar inside your cone and let the kids watch as these "stuffed feelings" blow the head off your clay person. Remind students that stuffed feelings can do that to us. But it doesn't have to be like that! We can express our feelings in many healthy and appropriate ways.

Bring out the box in which you have placed the following items: a prayer journal, pillow, box of tissues, running shoes, writing paper and pens, drawing paper and markers, a telephone directory, and a large red heart. Take out one item at a time and hand it to a class member, asking that person to think of how he could use the item to express his feelings in a healthy and positive way.

1. Prayer journal—express your feelings to God.

2. Pillow—hit it when you are angry; cry into it when you are sad.

3. Telephone directory—call someone you trust and talk about your feelings.

4. Writing paper and pen—write a letter, keep a diary, or write a poem about what you are feeling.

5. Drawing paper and markers—draw how you feel.

6. Box of tissues—sometimes you just need to cry!

7. Running shoes—do something physical.

8. Large red heart—talk to someone you love; ask for a hug.

Place all items in the middle of the table and read the following sentences. Ask students to refer to your list of rules for expressing feelings as they consider how each character expressed his feelings inappropriately. Then ask several volunteers to each choose one item from the table that he or she would personally use to express their feelings in a similar situation.

1. Jamie's parents are getting a divorce. She is so upset by this announcement that she locks herself in her room and vows never to go to school or talk to anyone again. *(Isolating herself is like stuffing her feelings; she is hurting herself by cutting herself off from others who can give her the support she needs.)*

2. Jack is angry at his mom for not listening to him and sending him to his room for something he didn't do. He smashes his lamp and clock and rips the blankets off his bed. *(Destroying things is never an appropriate or helpful way to express feelings.)*

3. Beverly is so nervous about giving her book report in front

of the class that she tells her mom she is too sick to go to school. *(Lying never helps a situation, and staying home would only postpone her having to give the report.)*

4. When another boy at school teases Greg for being short, Greg punches him so hard that the boy's nose starts to bleed. *(Hurting another person is never an appropriate or helpful way to express feelings.)*

End this segment by reviewing today's guideline for managing feelings: "*All* my feelings need to be expressed in healthy and appropriate ways." Have kids say it once or twice as you write it on your "Important Guidelines for Managing My Feelings" poster from last week.

Step 3

Write today's key verse on the chalkboard and have kids repeat it several times. Use a memory verse game to help kids memorize the verse. Start erasing one word at a time until the verse is completely erased and kids can say it. End by reminding them that when they stuff their feelings, they are not being truthful in the inner parts. Instead, they can face their feelings —especially the difficult ones—and express them in the ways discussed earlier.

Materials
chalk, chalkboard, eraser, Bible

Take It to the Next Level

Ask kids to report on the use of their prayer journals this past week; begin by sharing something you wrote in yours. If you offered an incentive for bringing the journals back, award those as kids leave. Encourage those who did not fill one out to do so this week, reminding them that telling God our feelings is the best way we have to express our feelings appropriately.

Distribute extra copies of the prayer journal to those who do not have one, and let kids fill out a page at this time. Remind them that their journal entries are private, so they can be totally honest. When everyone is finished, let some students who feel comfortable doing so to share something from their entries with the rest of the class.

For your closing prayer time, gather the kids into a tight circle and tell them you are about to have a little different prayer time. Have one student begin by praying, "God, thank you for giving me the feeling of _____ and for being with me when I feel _____." Go around the circle and let each student pray this sentence. Have them fill the blanks with some of the feelings mentioned today. Remind your students that this is a real prayer time and not just an exercise, so they are to take it seriously. End your prayer time by praying for your students.

Materials
your prayer journal, extra prayer journals

What Was That All About?

Cast: Sara, Jackie

Scene 1: The girls are walking to school

Sara: *(excited)* Hi Jackie! Boy, am I glad to see you! I tried to call you last night, but you weren't home. Guess what? My mom said we could have a sleep over for my birthday next month! Who do you think we should invite?

Jackie: *(sadly)* I don't know who you're going to invite, but I won't be there.

Sara: What do you mean? You're my best friend!

Jackie: My dad told us last night that we have to move to Texas. We're leaving in two weeks.

Sara: *(stares at Jackie for a moment, then says happily)* Well, that's big news! Texas is pretty far from here, but you'll probably have a great time living there. Maybe you can even get your own horse!

Jackie: *(shocked)* Sara, you look happy that I'm moving! Don't you understand? We aren't going to be together anymore!

Sara: Hey, we'll still be able to call and write to each other.

What Was That All About?

Cast: Sara, Sara's mom

Scene 2: Sara at home that evening

Mom: Hi, Sara! How was school today?

Sara: Fine, Mom! Mrs. Jackson said I have the best handwriting in the whole class.

Mom: Good for you! Wash up for dinner; we're eating a little early tonight.

Sara: We are? Why?

Mom: Because I have to go to a baby shower tonight, and I want the dinner dishes all cleaned up before I go.

Sara: *(explodes)* No! You know I watch Crime Busters every day after school! Today's gonna be a great episode, and I want to see it!

Mom: You've seen all those episodes a thousand times! You can miss one night.

Sara: But, Mom! I want to watch my show! You can't change things around because of some dumb shower! This is my time, and I want it to be the way it always is! *(runs out crying)*

Mom: *(looks stunned)* What was that all about? I wonder if something happened at school today to upset her? *(calls after her)* Sara! Come here! I want to talk to you! *(Exits)*

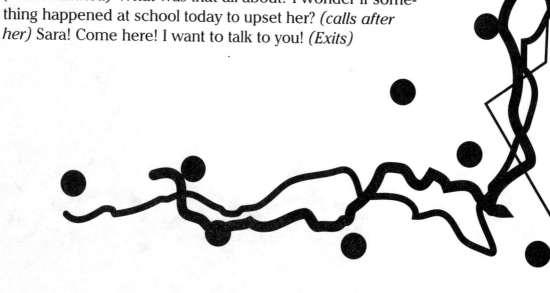

Session 3

Who's in Control Here?

Scripture: Jonah 1:1-17; 4:1; Matthew 27:1-5; Matthew 4:1-11; 1 Samuel 1:1-18
Key Verse: Philippians 4:6, 7

Guideline for Managing Feelings: I can be in control of my feelings rather than letting my feelings be in control of me!
Know four keys to staying in control of their feelings.
Feel empowered to handle confusing and overwhelming feelings.
Trust God to help them stay in control of their emotions.

Get Into the Game

As kids arrive, direct them to a table containing one or more baby name books, paper or poster board, glitter, glue, stickers, and pictures of sports, animals, and food. Instruct class members to make posters out of their names. They can begin by looking up the meaning of their names in the name book and printing their names in big letters in the center of their papers with its meaning printed underneath. Then they can choose materials from the table to personalize their posters. For instance, they can add stickers and pictures of their favorite color, food, pets, or sports. They can also add the names of family members, places they would like to visit, or what they want to be when them grow up. The point is for the finished poster to visually represent their uniqueness. When completed, have kids display their posters around the room.

Say, "Names are important. *Your* name is important! Your parents probably spent a long time choosing a name for you before you were born." Spend a few minutes discussing everyone's name posters. Emphasize the meaning of your kids' names and look for new information you can learn about their special interests.

Say, "Feelings have names, too. Just as your name is unique to you and your personality, every feeling has its own name and unique personality. Today we will talk about staying in control of our difficult feelings. As you will see, a big part of this is being able to call our feelings by their correct names. That's not as easy as it sounds. Have you ever had so many difficult feelings going on at once that you didn't really know what you were feeling? Today we will find out what to do when we feel that way."

Materials
a baby name book, white construction paper or poster board, stickers, glitter, glue, pictures of sports, animals, and food

Step 1

Begin by saying, "Sometimes our feelings get so mixed up that we become confused. At other times, our feelings are so intense that they feel overwhelming or frightening. We have to be careful during those times because when we don't know what to do about our confusing or overwhelming feelings, we can end up doing and saying things we really don't want to do or say. That's when our feelings take control of us. But God never intends for us to deal with our feelings in that way. He intends for us to use our feelings to live happy and safe lives. So what do we do when our feelings are confusing and overwhelming? Is there a way to control them? First let's see what we can learn from God's Word. Today we will look at some people in the Bible who experienced difficult feelings. Let's see what we can learn from the ways in which they handled those feelings."

Divide the class into four groups and give each group one of the "Search the Bible" assignments from page 35. Cut this sheet apart so each group gets only a copy of their own assignment. Give groups time to answer the questions and prepare a short skit to present during Step 2. (Note: If your class is small, use assignments 1 *or* 2 and 3 *or* 4 only.) Check on each group's work, guiding them to come to the following conclusions:

1. Jonah 1:1-17; 4:1. Jonah must have been feeling many things, including fear, guilt, remorse, and anger. His initial response was to run away—an unhealthy and inappropriate response to difficult feelings. Jonah let his feelings control his actions, and he ended up making an unwise and unhealthy choice!

2. Matthew 27:1-5. Judas felt remorse (deep guilt) for what he had done. This feeling was so overwhelming that he hung himself! Clearly, Judas let his feelings control his actions, and it cost him his life.

3. Matthew 4:1-11. Jesus must have had many feelings while he was in the desert; even though He was the Son of God, He was also fully human. He probably struggled with feeling hungry, lonely, and even tempted to give in to the devil's offers. Jesus handled all those difficult feelings by using Scripture verses to keep His perspective straight and to guide Him to make the right choices.

4. 1 Samuel 1:1-18. Being childless made Hannah feel sad at not fulfilling her role as a wife. She was not only tormented by her own feelings, but was wounded by harassment from her husband's other wife, who had successfully given him children. Rather than lashing out or trying to hurt the woman, Hannah stayed in control of her feelings by taking them to God and praying for His help.

Materials
photocopies of page 35 cut apart, Bibles

Step 2

Introduce the Bible skits. Say, "We will look at four people in the Bible and see how they handled their feelings. As you watch the skits, think about whether the people were in control of their feelings, or let their feelings control them." Invite the groups to make their presentations, being sure the information in Step 1 is clearly presented.

Summarize the skits by saying, "As you can see, even people in the Bible did not have an easy time managing their feelings. When our feelings seem confusing or overwhelming, it is easy to let them take control of our actions. When we aren't aware that's happening, we can make foolish choices and get into trouble. Instead we need a plan to help us when our feelings begin to take control of us."

Display the locked container in which you have placed snack-sized *Mars* bars with the words of Philippians 4:6, 7 taped to them. Place four keys on the table as you talk about each of the following guidelines.

Key #1—Stop and think. When our feelings seem confusing or overwhelming, our biggest temptation is to act too quickly. What are some signals that tell us we need to stop and think? *(having a big knot in our stomachs; wanting to do something hurtful or destructive, such as run away as Jonah did, or punch someone or break something.)*

Key #2—Name the feeling. First we need to think about exactly what we are feeling. It may seem simple, but calling our feelings by the correct names makes them less confusing and overwhelming! For instance, rather than saying, "I feel yucky," it's better to say something specific such as, "I'm angry that my best friend told my secret to the whole class," or "I'm scared to take the math test today because I forgot to study," or "I feel sad because I miss a good friend who moved away."

Key #3—Make a wise choice. When we stop and think before acting and can name our feeling, then we can wisely choose how to handle our feelings. That's what it means to be in control of our feelings rather than letting our feelings control us; not that we don't feel the feelings, but that we can make a wise choice about how to express them.

Key #4—Ask God to help. This is probably the most important key of all! Remember how Jesus handled His feelings? *(He remembered Bible verses to help him make a wise choice to resist the devil's temptations.)* How did Hannah handle her feelings? *(She kept praying about them and waited for God to help her.)* Since God gave us our feelings, He is certainly the best One to help us use them wisely.

Open the container with a key and take out the candy bars

Materials
words from the memory verse taped to snack-sized *Mars* bars, a container that locks, flour, keys, feelings poster from previous sessions, marker

with the words of Philippians 4:6, 7 on them. (If your class is large, make two sets.) Since this verse was also the key verse in **Session 1,** place the coins in the middle of the table and let the kids practice putting them in the right order. Then have kids read the verse together several times. Distribute the candy bars. Allow students to eat them as a snack or take them home.

End this segment by reviewing today's guideline for managing feelings: "I can be in control of my feelings rather than letting them be in control of me!" Have kids say it once or twice as you write it on your "Important Guidelines for Managing My Feelings" poster from last week.

Step 3

Say, "As we've seen today, having strong feelings can be confusing or overwhelming—or both! However, if we let our feelings take control during those times, we are in danger of making hurtful choices to try to cover them up or feel better. But with God's help, we can control our feelings and make wise choices to handle them."

Materials
paper, pens or pencils, small prizes (optional)

Divide the class into teams of four members each. Give each team paper and a pen or pencil. Then read the following questions, having each team discuss and record their answers without letting the other teams hear them. When all the responses have been recorded, start at the top and read the questions again, asking each team to read their responses. Award one point for each answer a team has on its list that no other team has. For example, if two teams listed anger as a response to number one, those answers cancel each other out. But if only one team listed guilt, that team scores a point. Encourage kids to think creatively so they can come up with responses the other teams did not think of. (Optional: Award a small prize to the team with the most points.)

1. a. What feelings would you have if your parents got a divorce? *(angry, guilty, sad, abandoned, afraid)*

b. What might you do in response if you let your feelings be in control of you? *(run away, break something, take it out on a sibling or friend, skip school)*

c. What could you do to handle your feelings in ways that would let you control them? *(talk to someone you trust, write a letter to your parents about your feelings, go to a support group)*

2. a. What feelings would you face if you failed a big history test that you had studied for really hard? *(like a failure, guilty, afraid to tell parent, embarrassed, angry, discouraged)*

b. What might you do if you let your feelings be in control of you? *(tear up the paper and hope your parents don't find out, give up and never study for a history test again, try to cheat on the next test to make up for it, kick your dog, yell at your little sister)*

c. What could you do to handle your feelings in ways that would let you control them? *(talk to your parents about how hard history is for you, ask the teacher for extra help)*

3. a. How would you feel if your best friend decided to have a party and did not invite you? *(abandoned, angry, confused, hurt, sad, lonely, vengeful)*

b. What might you do to handle your feelings if you let your feelings control you? *(try to sabotage the party, get revenge by hurting your friend in some way, never speak to your friend again, stuff your feelings)*

c. What could you do to handle your feelings in ways that would let you control them? *(ask your friend what's going on, talk to someone you trust about how hurt you feel, look for another best friend.)*

4. a. How would you feel if you went to a party and discovered all the kids were drinking beer? *(scared, pressured, disappointed, disgusted, angry, lonely)*

b. What might you do to handle your feelings if you let your feelings control you? *(drink to fit in, sit in a corner and try to survive until the party was over)*

c. What could you do to handle your feelings in ways that would let you control them? *(call your parents and ask them to pick you up, leave on your own if you can walk home, look for someone who is not drinking and leave together, tell an adult what happened)*

5. a. How would you feel if you got suspended from school for something another kid did? *(angry, betrayed, unheard, afraid, discouraged, embarrassed, lonely)*

b. What might you do to handle your feelings if you let your feelings be in control of you? *(get back at the kid who was guilty, cause more trouble in school to get back at the teacher who wouldn't listen to you, stop caring about doing well in school, try to hide from the other kids)*

c. What could you do to handle your feelings in ways that would let you control them? *(talk to your parents about what happened calmly and without blaming, try to tell your side of the story to the principal when everyone has calmed down, do something physical to release your anger)*

Conclude by reminding kids that dealing with strong feelings is never easy, but they can take control of their feelings by remembering to stop, think, and make a wise choice whenever their feelings start to control them.

Take It to the Next Level

Ask kids to report on using their prayer journals at home this past week; begin by sharing yours with the class. If you offered a small incentive for bringing journals back, award those as kids leave today. Encourage those who did not fill out their journal to do so this week, reminding them that our best way to express feelings in healthy and appropriate ways is to express them to God.

Distribute extra photocopies of the prayer journal to those who do not have one and allow time for kids to fill out a page. Ask them to focus today's entry on a particular feeling that may be difficult to handle and the situation producing it. Ask them to think about the following questions to help them make a choice:

1. Are you afraid to do something, or afraid something will happen?

2. Has something happened to make you sad, or do you miss anyone very much?

3. Did someone do something you are angry about, or did something happen to make you angry?

4. Did you do something you feel guilty about?

5. Do you feel lonely at home or at school?

6. Do you feel abandoned by a family member or friend you thought would always be there for you?

Give students a few minutes to write a prayer in their journals, asking for God's help in managing a difficult feeling and the situation producing it. Then lead the kids in prayer.

Materials
your prayer journal, extra prayer journals

Search the Bible

Group 1

1. Read Jonah 1:1-17; 4:1.
2. Answer these questions:
   - What feelings do you think Jonah faced?
   - What did Jonah do about his feelings?
   - Was Jonah in control of his feelings or did he let his feelings control him?
3. Prepare a simple skit to present this story to the rest of the class.

Group 2

1. Read Matthew 27:1-5.
2. Answer these questions:
   - What feelings did Judas have?
   - What did Judas do about his feelings?
   - Was Judas in control of his feelings or did he let his feelings control him?
3. Prepare a simple skit to present this story to the rest of the class.

Group 3

1. Read Matthew 4:1-11.
2. Answer these questions:
   - What do you think Jesus felt?
   - What did Jesus do to stay in control of His feelings?
   - Did Jesus control His feelings or did He let His feelings control Him?
3. Prepare a simple skit to present this story to the rest of the class.

Group 4

1. Read 1 Samuel 1:1-18.
2. Answer these questions:
   - What did Hannah feel?
   - What did Hannah do about her feelings?
   - Was Hannah in control of her feelings or did she let her feelings control her?
3. Prepare a simple skit to present this story to the rest of the class.

Session 4

Danger Ahead!

Scripture: Galatians 5:19-26; Ephesians 4:31, 32; 6:10, 11; Colossians 3:8-17
Key Verse: Ephesians 4:26, 27

Guideline for Managing Feelings: With God's Spirit in my heart, rage, bitterness, jealousy, and envy won't have a chance to start!
Know that rage, bitterness, jealousy, and envy are strong feelings that can easily lead to destructive actions.
Feel alert and prepared to handle difficult feelings when they arise.
Use prayer as a defense against rage, bitterness, jealousy, and envy.

Get Into the Game

As students arrive, direct them to tables on which you have set a large quantity of items that would be considered junk: scraps of paper, empty cans and boxes, bits of yarn or string, old buttons, dried leaves, twigs, old costume jewelry, and so on. Instruct kids that their task is to create something beautiful from things that, by themselves, we would say are junk or useless. They can use any means they like to create a junk sculpture. (Optional: Let the kids know you will judge the sculptures and award prizes for various categories such as best use of large pieces, best use of small pieces, used the most pieces, looks most like a recognizable object such as a car, house, horse, and so on.)

When kids have finished their sculptures, direct them to another table containing magazine pictures of endangered animals, rain forests, kids on drugs, floods, and fires. Instruct them to use pictures and words to make a poster of how something that was once beautiful was transformed into something ugly. When complete, display the posters around the room.

Say, "We've spent some time today doing two things. First, we took things that we would normally call ugly or useless and turned them into sculptures that have some beauty. Then we looked at things that had been created as beautiful but were transformed into something ugly. Today we will see how the same things can happen with our feelings. Although God created all our feelings and means for them to help us live safe and enjoyable lives, certain feelings are so powerful they can easily become destructive and ugly. We will also see how God can transform those feelings into something beautiful again when we ask Him!"

Materials
scrap paper, empty pop cans, old boxes, dried up leaves, twigs, old jewelry, glue, magazine pictures of endangered animals, rain forests, kids on drugs, floods, and fires, small prizes (optional)

Step 1

Display a poster board on which you have written, "Alien Forces." Divide the board into three columns, labeling the first one Dangerous Feelings, the second Defender Feelings, and the third Guidelines. Then distribute the feeling words cards evenly among your students. Ask them to look at their cards. If they think they have a dangerous feeling word, they can place it in the middle of the table. Then ask volunteers to read the following references. After each, have students attach the cards to the poster with the feelings mentioned in these verses: Galatians 5:19-21; Ephesians 4:31; Colossians 3:8. *(Feelings mentioned include anger, rage, envy, hatred, jealousy, selfishness, bitterness, and revenge.)*

Say, "These feelings are very powerful, and God has warned us not to let them take control of our lives. If we ignore this warning, they can lead us to do hurtful and destructive things to ourselves and others. On the other hand, God has also given us some defender feelings. Let's see what else we can learn about these from God's Word." Have students read the following verses, placing the feelings mentioned in the second column: Galatians 5:22, 23; Ephesians 4:32; Colossians 3:12-14. *(Feelings mentioned include love, joy, patience, humility, kindness, gentleness, forgiveness, compassion, joy, and peace.)*

Say, "These feelings are called defenders because they and the dangerous feelings cannot exist in our lives at the same time. In other words, we cannot have hatred and love at the same time because love will destroy hatred. So, by growing God's defender feelings in our lives, we are protecting ourselves from the potentially destructive ones."

Materials
3" x 5" cards with feeling words from the Unit Introduction written on them, white poster board, marker, Bibles

Step 2

Say, "When we first started talking about feelings, I said that all our feelings are OK and that God created *all* of them to help us live healthy and safe lives. Now it sounds as if I'm saying something different, doesn't it? Actually, having feelings such as rage, envy, jealousy, and bitterness is not the problem. Sometimes we will all feel these; that's part of being human. What we do when we start to feel them is what's important. Let me show you what I mean."

Display your basket containing several pieces of rotten fruit and pictures of a flood, a house on fire, and a tornado. Ask a student to reach inside and take out one of the items. Let other students remove items until all of the items are on the table. Then talk about each one, pointing out the fact that none of these items are ugly or destructive. A banana and an orange,

Materials
basket containing several pieces of rotten fruit, pictures of a flood, a house on fire, and a tornado, poster of Ephesians 4:26, 27, several pieces of fresh fruit, picture of a science fiction weapon (i.e. light saber, phaser gun, etc.), "Guidelines for Managing My Feelings" poster, marker

for example, are good things that we need in order to live a healthy life. But when we keep them too long, they get rotten. To eat them at that stage would harm us. Likewise, refer to the picture of the house on fire, the flood, and the tornado. These things are simply fire, water, and wind. All of them are good in and of themselves, but when they get out of control they become destructive. In the same way, when we let powerful feelings such as anger grow inside of us too long, they can become very destructive.

Display a poster of today's key verse, Ephesians 4:26, 27, and have kids read it together. Say, "Notice that this verse does *not* say that being angry is wrong; it warns us not to do something hurtful or destructive when we feel angry. Then it gives us a great guideline for how to avoid letting anger become destructive. What is that guideline?" Guide students to see that by quickly working out whatever is making us angry, we diffuse the anger before it can turn into rage or bitterness. Then write "Work it out" in the Guidelines column of the Alien Forces poster.

Say, "God has given us more guidelines." Ask a volunteer to read Galatians 5:22 again. Add "Grow God's Fruit of the Spirit" to your poster. Then add several pieces of fresh fruit to your basket. Remind kids that when the fruit of the Spirit is growing in our lives, the dangerous feelings will be neutralized.

Next, have a volunteer read Ephesians 6:10, 11. Add "Put on God's Armor" to the poster. If you have one, add a picture of a science fiction weapon (i.e. light saber, phaser gun, etc.) to your basket as you say, "Just as a science fiction hero will use certain items to stay safe and help him accomplish his task, in the same way God has given us His protective gear to help us stay safe. That means we can depend on God to give us the protection and power we need to handle feelings such as rage, envy, bitterness, and jealousy before they have a chance to grow into a destructive force." Have kids say the three guidelines together. "All these guidelines are powerful spiritual weapons that God gives us to keep potentially destructive feelings from taking control of us."

End this segment by reviewing your "Important Guidelines for Managing My Feelings" poster from past weeks. Add today's guideline to the poster: "With God's Spirit in my heart, rage, bitterness, jealousy, and envy won't have a chance to start!"

Step 3

Place a small container of oil and another of water on your table. Offer to give $10 to any student who can mix the two together in such a way that they will not separate. Let anyone

Materials
small containers of oil and water, masking tape, photocopies of page 41

who wants to try. Then use masking tape to make an X on the floor. Choose two students and tell them you will give them $10 if they can both stand on the exact middle of the X at the same time. Your students will quickly see that it is impossible to accomplish either task: oil and water cannot mix together and two objects cannot share the same space at the same time. Say, "This is an illustration of what we're trying to say today about letting God's fruit of the Spirit protect you from potentially destructive feelings. When God places His love in your heart, bitterness cannot also be there. When God's peace grows in you, envy cannot hurt you. And when you have God's gentleness in your life, rage will be pushed out. Of course, growing the fruit of the Spirit in our lives is not as easy as it sounds. A big part of it comes through praying for God to do His work in our hearts. But we must also be aware of how the choices we make either let the Spirit of God grow in us or keep the Spirit from growing His fruit in us."

Distribute photocopies of page 41. Let kids work individually or in pairs to design a cartoon illustrating how their powerful feelings can lead them into destructive actions. Guide them into the activity with the following directions.

1. Look at the first frame in which the boy is angry. Who do you think the adult is? *(possibly a parent, teacher, or neighbor?)* What do you think happened to cause his anger? *(could be a conflict with the adult or it could be another conflict that the boy is simply reporting to the adult)*

2. In the second frame, the boy is alone. What choices will he consider to express his anger? Write a different choice in each dialogue bubble. *(Break something? Hit someone? Stuff it? Get revenge?)*

3. In the third frame, draw the boy acting out his final choice.

4. In the last frame, draw the results of the boy's choice. *(a fight, sent to the principal's office, or grounded)*

Ask kids to share their cartoons with each other. Then distribute another photocopy of the cartoon sheet and ask kids to repeat the process, this time illustrating what choices the boy could make in the same situation if he has God's fruit of the Spirit growing in his heart. Have them share these cartoons with each other. If time permits, ask for volunteers to act out their stories for the rest of the class.

Take It to the Next Level

Ask kids to report on using their prayer journals at home this past week; begin by sharing yours with the class. If you offered a small incentive for bringing the journals back, award those as kids are leaving today.

Materials
your prayer journal, extra prayer journals, photocopies of page 42

Distribute extra photocopies of the prayer journal to those who do not have one and let kids fill out a page at this time. Ask them to focus today's entry on asking God to grow the fruit of the Spirit in them. They can choose the one that seems to be hardest for them to grow, and write a prayer asking for God's help in that area of their lives.

End your time by making a class book of prayers. Prepare students by saying, "In the past few weeks we have learned many things about the feelings God has placed within us. We've learned that they are a valuable gift from the Lord to help us live enjoyable and safe lives. We've also learned that they can be difficult to manage and even potentially destructive, but that expressing them honestly to God and asking for His help is the best tool we have to handle our feelings well. Today we are going to make a book of prayers. As you share your deepest feelings with God, you can actually help another person who may have the same feelings as you. Take a few minutes to quietly write a prayer to the Lord. Then we will put all our prayers together into our book."

Distribute photocopies of page 42 and ask kids to individually write their prayers. When all are finished, collect them and bind them into a class book of prayers. Make photocopies during the week and send them to the kids so they can each have one at home.

When you have collected all the prayers, stand in a circle and hold hands. Pray for your students, asking God to protect them from the potentially destructive feelings of rage, envy, bitterness, and jealousy by filling them with the fruit of the Spirit and clothing them with His spiritual armor.

Growing God's Fruit of the Spirit

Bridge the Gap
Family Feelings

Scripture: Ephesians 4:26, 27, 29-32

Know which words and actions produce positive feelings and which destroy family peace and unity.
Feel motivated to decrease the words and actions that produce negative feelings and increase the ones that bring about family unity and peace.
Choose one strategy to actively increase positive feelings in their family.

You will need to plan well in advance of this session to accomplish the following tasks.

1. Prepare for the Exploration Mission. This session opens with a variation on the scavenger hunt. First, fill a metal box with snack-sized *Mars* candy bars with feelings words from the Unit Introduction taped onto them, photocopies of "Building Family Unity" on page 47, and a scroll containing the key Scripture passage, Ephesians 4:26, 27, 29-32. This will function as your time capsule.

Prior to the session, hide the time capsule somewhere inside or outside of the church (i.e. behind a bush, underneath a pew, in the choir loft). Of course, depending on when you are conducting this session, be sure to get permission to do this so you will not disrupt any other activities.

Should you decide to give the family teams more direction, give each team a written cryptic message (i.e. in a galaxy inside, in a galaxy outside, near the outer limits of your universe, etc.).

2. Invite a guest to lead families in the goal-setting activity. The last activity of this session involves families in setting a goal to increase the positive feelings in their homes. Invite a family life educator, a family therapist, or one of your ministers who works with families to join you for this time. Ask the person to make a short presentation giving practical suggestions for managing feelings in family life. Then lead the families in a goal setting activity. Ask the guest to prepare a worksheet to guide the families through the goal-setting process. Get this in advance so you can prepare the copies.

Get Into the Game

This activity requires advance preparation! Follow the directions at the beginning of this session carefully to get ready for the exploration mission.

As families arrive, give everyone a name tag. Then introduce the exploration mission saying, "During each week of this session, we have discovered new insights about our feelings. Today, we will discover how our feelings affect our families. But first we have to find a time capsule I have hidden somewhere nearby."

Explain the rules of the mission and answer all questions. Distribute any clues you may have prepared and send families off to find the capsule. Reconvene your session when all have returned. Allow the winning team to read the feeling words taped to the candy bars and distribute them for all to enjoy.

Materials
name tags, time capsule containing items listed at the beginning of this session

Step 1

Place the time capsule in the center of your group. Say, "In weeks past, we have used items that have helped us learn about our feelings. We have learned that all our feelings are important—even the ones we don't like to feel. We've learned to express our feelings in healthy and safe ways. Finally, we learned that some feelings are more dangerous than others; feelings such as rage, envy, and bitterness can become destructive if we don't deal with them properly. Today we will learn about managing feelings in our family lives. Let's start in the same place we always do—in the Bible."

Open your time capsule and remove the scroll. Have the whole group read the verses together. Say, "These verses are particularly helpful in managing our family. We would like to think that our families *always* experience love, forgiveness, kindness, and compassion, and no one ever uses unkind words or feels rage, envy, or bitterness. Does any family here live like that all the time? Of course not, because our families are made up of humans who get angry and envious and sometimes say unkind things. So today we want to talk about how to manage the feelings in our families, how to make the positive ones grow, and how to control the ones that hurt our families."

Give families a few minutes to talk together, asking them to answer the question, "What practical things can we learn from

Materials
Bibles, scroll of Ephesians 4:26, 27, 29-32

these verses that will help us accomplish this goal?" Ask them to apply the verses to specific instances in their family lives. For instance, instead of saying, "Don't go to bed angry," parents could say, "When we have a disagreement and send you to your room, we need to come in and talk about what happened after all of us have had a chance to cool down." Or a preteen could say, "I know I'm not kind to my sister; I can do that better." Don't be concerned if families have trouble with this at first; you will be giving them practical help to carry out the teachings of these verses as the session continues.

After a short time of discussion, ask families to share any insights they gained with the rest of the group.

Step 2

Say, "Some of you may have figured out already that a big part of how we feel in our families is connected to how we act toward each other. In other words, when we say kind words to each other and treat each other with respect, kindness, and forgiveness, we have good feelings. Of course, the opposite is also true; when we say unkind things to each other and let rage, envy, and bitterness determine our actions, it will be very hard to have a peaceful, united family. Here's the key concept we want to talk about today: Every family has specific words and actions that cause family peace and unity, or specific words and actions that destroy it. Those specific words and actions will be different for each family."

Distribute photocopies of page 47 and pens or pencils to all participants. Give them a few minutes to fill out the top section individually, not letting other family members see their responses. Remind them to fill in the blanks with *specific* words and actions (i.e. when you do your chores without being reminded, when we go on family outings, when you say "I love you" and give me a big hug before I go to sleep, when you take the time to come to my activities).

After a few minutes, have family members get together and share their responses with each other. Finally, ask families to share any discoveries they made with the whole group.

Materials
photocopies of page 47, pens or pencils

Step 3

Say, "It certainly would be great if we could have positive feelings in our families all the time! But we know life is not like that."

Direct participants to the bottom portion of their activity sheets. Give them a few minutes to fill out this section individually, not letting other family members see their responses.

Remind them to fill in the blanks with specific words and actions that they feel destroy peace and unity in their families (i.e. when you tell me I can't do anything right, when you're always too busy to listen to me or come to my activities, when I call you and you just ignore me, when you fight and don't get along.)

After a few minutes, have families share their responses with each other. Finally, ask families to share their discoveries about how any specific words and actions they may have been unaware of were actually sabotaging their family peace and unity.

Take It to the Next Level

Invite your special speaker to make his presentation to your families at this time. The objective is to guide families to set one specific goal that will allow them to *reduce* destructive words and behaviors and *increase* the positive words and actions that enhance family peace and unity. Your speaker should be prepared to teach families how to set a goal that all family members can work together to achieve and use a family goal-setting activity sheet to guide families through this exercise.

End your session by leading participants in a guided prayer time. Ask participants to pray silently as you direct them:
1. Thank God for one special thing about your family.
2. Tell God about the goal you just set.
3. Ask God to help you do your part to achieve your goal.
4. Praise God for taking care of your family's needs throughout the years.

Close with a prayer, asking God to help all participants find one new way to strengthen their relationships at home during the coming week.

Materials
guest speaker you've contacted in advance, photocopies of activity sheets prepared by the guest speaker

Part 1:
Words and actions that *bring* peace and unity to our family

Fill in the blanks with specific words other family members say
and specific actions they do that make you feel the following feelings:

I feel LOVE in my family when _____.

I feel PROUD of my family when _____.

I feel EXCITED in my family when _____.

I feel HAPPY in my family when _____.

I feel PEACEFUL in my family when _____.

I feel KINDNESS in my family when _____.

Part 2:
Words and actions that *destroy* peace and unity to our family

Fill in the blanks with specific words other family members say
and specific actions they do that make you feel the following feelings:

I feel ANGRY in my family when _____.

I feel LONELY in my family when _____.

I feel SAD in my family when _____.

I feel AFRAID in my family when _____.

I feel ASHAMED in my family when _____.

I feel UNLOVED in my family when _____.

Go to Extremes
I Feel for You!

Scripture: Philippians 2:4, 5; 2 Corinthians 1:3, 4

Know that many preteens experience difficult life circumstances making it hard for them to experience happiness and joy.
Feel a desire to help kids living in such circumstances.
Participate in a project to offer support and caring to kids who are hurting or in need.

This session will involve your students in a service project to offer help and support to kids who live with some of life's most painful circumstances. Prior to this session, you will need to find possible projects your kids can do. We've provided a list of suggestions, but feel free to research other possibilities in your church or community. Make your preparations well enough in advance so you can invite several representatives to raise your class awareness about kids in need. Ask representatives to bring pictures of the kids they work with and anything else that will help your preteens comprehend what life is like for the kids these agencies serve. Here are some examples of possible projects:

   1. Homeless Children. Many homeless shelters house families with children. If you have a homeless shelter in your area, check with them to see how many children are staying in the shelter and if someone is available to speak to your class. Also ask your class to do a project to get your students personally involved. Shelters often need personal items such as soap, toothpaste, toys, or children's books. Your class could put together age appropriate packets containing these items and deliver them to the kids in the shelter. Some shelters may even let you plan a party for their kids.
   2. Children of Prisoners. Several organizations minister to the needs of prisoners' families. Children in these families have

many needs, including basics such as food and clothes. A representative could introduce your preteens to what life is like for these kids and suggest ways your class could help. One possibility may be to write letters to the kids, starting some pen pal relationships.

3. Children around the world. Agencies such as World Vision, Feed the Children, or Compassion International will always send representatives to speak to your class. They will have lots of pictures and ideas to familiarize your class to children with lifestyles very different from their own. They may also be able to suggest service projects.

4. Check with your congregation. Your church leadership may know of other community agencies or churches in your area that would welcome a chance to speak to your kids, and would possibly involve them in a service project to needy kids in your community.

Get Into the Game

Before kids arrive, prepare a set of cards with feeling words written on them. Choose about twenty words from the list of feeling words on page 14 that the kids can easily act out. As kids arrive, place them in pairs and give one person in each pair a card. That person must then act out the feeling, using only body movements. The partner's job is to act as the reflection in a mirror, do exactly the same movements, and then guess what the feeling word is. When the word has been guessed, have the partners switch roles and draw a new card.

Say, "Today we are going to shift our emphasis just a bit. So far, we have been learning how to be aware of and manage our own feelings. Today we want to talk about how to recognize and respond to other people's feelings."

Materials
feeling words written on index cards

Step 1

Ask a volunteer to read Philippians 2:4, 5 and 2 Corinthians 1:3, 4. Ask, "In light of our discussions about feelings, what do these two passages tell us?" Guide kids to see that God teaches us to be concerned for the needs of others, which means paying attention to what others around us are feeling and responding with caring and sensitivity.

Say, "It is easy for us to be concerned with our own interests, needs, and feelings. But God says that we are to care for other people's interests and needs, just as Jesus did. We must care about what other people are feeling and reach out to them. The verses in 2 Corinthians talk about offering comfort to

Materials
Bibles

people who need it. That is just one example of how we can reach out to people when we pay attention to what they may feel. We call this sensitivity, or empathy, and we can all develop these qualities."

Step 2

Say, "Today I have invited several guests to help us learn more about reaching out to others with sensitivity and empathy. These people will help you learn about some kids whose lives are very different from your own. Many of those kids seldom experience safe or happy feelings. Yet these are children God cares for very deeply, and He asks us to care for them, too."

Invite your guests to make their presentations at this time. Include time for questions.

Materials
representatives from various organizations

Step 3

Take this time to present to your kids the actual project they will do. Discuss ways of raising money, if needed, writing letters, or preparing packets for kids in a homeless shelter. Prepare with enthusiasm. By doing so, your students will get a real sense that by participating in this project, they will be performing a significant ministry to kids who experience some of life's most difficult feelings.

Materials
any items needed to prepare for your class service project

Take It to the Next Level

Complete your preparations by discussing the details of when and how you will actually carry out the project if you did not complete it today. For instance, if you are going to a homeless shelter, tell the kids when and where, etc. Be sure to send parent letters home with the kids. These letters should contain a complete description of the project, including times and dates. A permission slip to be signed and returned to you has been provided on page 51. Make photocopies of that page for every student in your class.

Materials
photocopies of page 51

Permission Slip

Preteen's Name _____

Address _____

Birthdate _____ Phone _____

Emergency person & phone _____

    A parent's signature below signifies consent for the named preteen to travel and participate in activities with the _____ Church. It also signifies that in the event of an emergency and if the parent cannot be contacted at the above listed phone number, the parent gives the staff and/or the sponsors of _____ Church permission to act on the parent's behalf.

    A parent's signature also signifies that in the case of an accident, the parent releases _____ Church staff, leadership, and sponsors from liability. The parent's signature also indicates that it is the parent's responsibility to pay any medical bills that might be incurred as the result of a medical emergency.

Signed _____ Date _____

Insurance Company & Account Number _____

    Please list any medical allergies, medications being taken, medical problems, or other pertinent information.

_____

_____

_____

Unit 2
Trust Trek

Trust is an everyday part of our lives. We trust the alarm clock to sound at the very minute to which we set it the night before. We trust water to flow from the faucet as we step into the shower. We trust our car to start when we turn the key. We trust the air we breath to be oxygen rather than carbon monoxide.

We also trust people. We trust policemen to maintain the laws of our city and state. We trust our spouses to be faithful. We trust our bosses to evaluate us fairly. Trust is at the heart of every relationship.

Your preteen students are trying to understand what trust is, who they can trust, who they can't trust, and why. Some of your students may have a friend who has not been loyal to them. Some of your students may have experienced unfairness from a coach. Some of your students may be living through their parents' divorce. Some of your students may have been lied to. Some of your students may have been abused by someone they love.

These sessions will help your students understand trust and build trusting relationships with other kids, adults, and especially God. As they investigate trust in many types of relationships, the students will desire to have meaningful relationships that are based on trust. They will see that the beginning of having these kinds of relationships is being trustworthy themselves. Trust can break down in relationships. Some of your students have experienced the pain of this breakdown. Students will discover when and how to rebuild trust.

The most important relationship ever built on trust is one with God. Your students will work on building a trusting relationship with Him.

The students will study the life of David as they make discoveries about trust. David demonstrated his trustworthiness. He also demonstrated his struggle with trust. David was a man after God's own heart; he had a significant relationship with God. And David had a valuable relationship with Jonathan, one that exemplifies trust in many ways. David also had some trust issues. He trusted King Saul, yet King Saul tried to kill him several times. God trusted David, yet David committed adultery with Bathsheba and then had her husband killed. As the students study David, they will compare his struggles and victories with trust to their own.

Unit aims

Know how to have trusting relationships.
Feel convicted to build trusting relationships.
Work on building trust in relationships with others and with God.

Session 1—Blast Off
The students will define trust, recognize the trait in various situations, and begin to work on being trustworthy.
Know the definition of trust.
Feel convicted to build trusting relationships.
Work on being trustworthy.

Session 2—Trusting Comrades
The students will identify trust in various types of relationships—with parents, with friends, with authority figures—and begin to work on building trust in those relationships.
Know how to have trusting relationships.
Feel convicted to build trusting relationships.
Work on building trust in relationships.

Session 3—You're Breaking Up . . .
Students will identify how trust can be broken in a relationship and develop action steps to rebuild trust when appropriate.
Know what to do when a relationship's trust is broken.
Feel convicted to build trusting relationships.
Work on rebuilding trust in a relationship.

Session 4—Trust Trek With God
Students will recognize the importance of their relationship

with God. They will begin to build a personal relationship with Him.
Know how to trust God.
Feel convicted to build trusting relationships.
Work on building a trusting relationship with God.

Bridge the Gap—Trust Trek Trip
This special family session is designed to be a trust experience for the entire family. Family members of all ages will build trust in their family unit through trust experiments, games, role plays, and prayer.

Go to Extremes—A Prayer Walk
This service project is designed for students to tell what they have learned about trust and to emphasize prayer. The prayer walk is an event involving worship and prayer as a whole group, followed by stations centering on specific focuses.

Unit projects

Games
Encourage students to play some familiar games in pairs. For example, have a pair of students use a *Jenga* type game to build a tower with another student pair. The students will have to work together to make decisions. They will have to cooperate and trust one another, especially if one is more skilled at the game than the other. Some games to try: *Uno*, checkers, chess, solitaire, or any board game.

Trust studies
Instruct students to research people who trusted God. The people could be Bible characters—Abraham, Moses, Paul, Peter. The people could be historical figures such as Martin Luther King or Corrie Ten Boom. The people could be contemporary Christians—Dave Dravecky, Billy Graham, James Dobson. Or the students could research people they know. Encourage the students to gather information about the person they are studying and prepare the research material for the class to see. A student could write an essay, make a scrapbook, or interview someone on video.

Trust Trek Scrapbook
Instruct students to make a scrapbook of people they trust and why. A student may want to make a traditional scrapbook in an album, or a video scrapbook—videotaping segments of them talking to each person they trust. A student could create a scrapbook on a computer.

Daily Devotions

Use these Scriptures as a study guide in your own personal devotion time.

Week One Be Trustworthy	Week Two Trust Others	Week Three Trust Again	Week Four Trust God
Key verse to remember: Galatians 5:22, 23	**Key verse to remember:** 1 John 4:7, 8	**Key verse to remember:** Romans 8:37	**Key verse to remember:** Isaiah 8:17
Monday Example from David's life— 1 Samuel 16:1-13	**Monday** Example from David's life— 1 Samuel 18:1-4	**Monday** Example from David's life— 1 Samuel 19:1-7	**Monday** Example from David's life— Acts 13:22
Tuesday Galatians 5:22, 23	**Tuesday** 1 John 4:7, 8	**Tuesday** Romans 8:37	**Tuesday** Proverbs 3:5, 6
Wednesday 2 Peter 1:5-7	**Wednesday** Matthew 22:36-39	**Wednesday** James 1:2-4	**Wednesday** Psalm 25:4, 5
Thursday Philippians 2:3, 4	**Thursday** 1 Corinthians 13	**Thursday** Proverbs 3:5, 6	**Thursday** Matthew 6:33
Friday Pray that God will help you be more trustworthy in your friendships.	**Friday** Pray that God will give you courage and guidance to build trusting relationships.	**Friday** Pray that God will help you rebuild a broken relationship when it is appropriate.	**Friday** Thank God for being trustworthy and reliable. Tell Him how important He is to you.

Session 1

Blast Off!

Scripture: various passages from 1 Samuel, 2 Samuel, 1 Kings

Know the definition of trust.
Feel convicted to build trusting relationships.
Work on being trustworthy.

Get Into the Game

Guide your students to participate in a trust experiment. This activity works best with ten to fifteen participants. If you have more than fifteen in your group, divide them into two groups.

Designate one person as *It*. The other students will stand in a circle shoulder to shoulder facing in. *It* stands in the center of the circle and crosses his arms across his chest.

It stiffens his body and falls backwards. The students in the circle catch him around the arms and shoulders and passes him to other students while his feet remain on the floor. Continue passing *It* around the circle several more times. This works best if *It* keeps his feet together and near the center of the circle.

Take turns until all the students have had a chance to be *It*.

Suggested discussion questions: Why was it hard to trust the other students? If they had dropped you, why would it be hard to trust them again?

Step 1

Activity #1

Before the session, write these Scripture references on index cards: 1 Samuel 16:1-13; 1 Samuel 16:19-23; 1 Samuel 17; 1 Samuel 18:1-4; 1 Samuel 18:5-11; 1 Samuel 19:1-7; 1 Samuel 19:8-10; 1 Samuel 19:11-17; 1 Samuel 20; 1 Samuel 23:7, 8, 13, 14, 16-18; 1 Samuel 24; 1 Samuel 26:7-12, 22-25; 1 Samuel 31:1-3; 1 Samuel 31:4, 5; 2 Samuel 2:1-4; 2 Samuel 6:1-12; 2 Samuel 9; 2 Samuel 11:2-5, 14-17, 26, 27; 2 Samuel 12:1-18, 24, 25; 1 Kings 1:28-30; 2:1-3, 10-12.

These Scripture passages give the highlights of David's life—

Materials
index cards, Bibles, miscellaneous props, poster board

all the way from shepherding his father's sheep to reigning as the king of Israel. Your students will prepare a way to retell the events of David's life to the rest of the class.

Divide students into pairs. Give each pair an index card with one Scripture passage written on it. Instruct the pairs to look up and read the Scripture passages. Give the longer passages to your better readers or students who comprehend the Bible well. Some pairs may take more than one passage if you have index cards left over. Or, if time is limited, you may want to retell the events of some passages yourself.

When the students have read the passages, guide each pair to develop a way to retell the Scripture passage to the class later in the session. One student pair may decide to draw what happened on a piece of poster board. One may want to act out the events of the Scripture passage—with or without words. One student pair may decide to read the shorter passages and have other students act out what happens. Give the students some freedom to express themselves with this activity.

A brief summary of David's life follows to help you draw out some of the important facts.

David is chosen by God and anointed by Samuel to succeed King Saul. David becomes an armor-bearer for Saul and moves to his house. Saul is often comforted by David's harp playing. David kills the great Philistine Goliath. Jonathan, Saul's son, befriends David. Saul tries to kill David repeatedly because he is jealous of David's success in battle and feels threatened by him. Jonathan talks to Saul on David's behalf several times. God protects David from King Saul. David has several opportunities to kill King Saul but he does not because he respects Saul's position as God's anointed king. Jonathan is killed in a battle by the Philistines. King Saul commits suicide, and David is crowned king of Judah. David plans to bring the Ark of the Covenant to Jerusalem. Uzzah dies when he touches the ark so David leaves it at Obed-Edom's house. He does eventually bring the ark to Jerusalem. David finds Mephibosheth, Jonathan's son, and brings him to Jerusalem to provide for him. David sleeps with Bathsheba, Uriah's wife, and she gets pregnant. David has her husband killed in battle to cover his sin. Nathan confronts David about his sin. David and Bathsheba's son dies. David and Bathsheba have Solomon. David, as he is dying, makes Solomon king.

Suggested discussion questions: How did David trust God? How did David trust Jonathan? How did David trust Saul?

Activity #2

Focus your students' attention on trust. Discuss what trust is and times that we trust. Look up the definition of trust in the

Materials
Play-Doh

dictionary (*assured reliance on the character, ability, strength, or truth of someone or something*).

Distribute handfuls of *Play-Doh* to the students. Instruct the students to use the *Play-Doh* and construct something they trust. Have the students work individually. Give them some examples of things that we trust every day.

• We trust clocks to show the accurate time.
• We trust alarm clocks to wake us in the morning.
• We trust cars and buses to take us where we are going.
• We trust the seams in our clothes to stay secure and not fall apart.
• We trust the sun to come up in the morning and to set at night.
• We trust the air we breath to be oxygen and not carbon monoxide.
• We trust the structure of multi-level homes to be safe.

The students will show their creations during Step 3 and talk about trust.

Suggested discussion questions: What is trust? How do we trust? Who do we trust? How has someone you trusted done something that makes you question your trust in him?

Activity #3

Photocopy the bottom portion of page 62 and distribute. Guide your students to prepare role plays. They will act out the case studies for the other students during Step 3.

• One of the rules at Lauren's house is to come straight home from school. Lauren is usually home after school for about an hour before her mom gets home from work. One day last week, Jessica asked Lauren to come home with her so she could show Lauren her new keyboard. Lauren really wanted to see the keyboard because she has been wanting one also. So she went with Jessica. She knew she had enough time to go to Jessica's house and be home before her mom got home from work. Her mom would never know.

• Aaron's parents talked to him over the weekend about a big change in his family. His parents were going to get a divorce. Not only were they not going to be together in one house anymore, but they wanted him to decided who he wanted to live with. Everything in his life was going to be different. He was really mad at both his mom and his dad. He didn't know what to do. When he got to church on Sunday morning he told his Sunday school teacher and class. They prayed for him. When he was leaving class he told his teacher that he felt a little better.

After the students have prepared their pantomimes, guide them to discuss the trust issues in each skit. For example, Lauren's mom trusts her to come home from school, but

Materials
photocopies of page 62

Lauren is not trustworthy when she goes to Jessica's house. John trusted his mom and dad, and he feels as if they have let him down. John shows trust in his teacher and class by telling them about his parents' divorce.

Suggested discussion questions: Why is Lauren not trustworthy? Will it be difficult for her mom to trust her if she found out what she did? Who does John trust? Has your trust in someone ever been broken?

Step 2

Ask the students who prepared Activity #2 to show their cardboard creations now. Ask them to tell about each item and talk about why we trust it. Guide them to define trust.

Ask the students to present their portions of David's life in chronological order. The narrative of his life begins in 1 Samuel 16, proceeds through 1 and 2 Samuel, and ends in 1 Kings 1. Following their presentations, discuss trust in general with your students. Tie in examples from David's life. Use the summary of David's life found under Activity #1 and the following examples of trust to focus your students' attention.

- David's dad trusted him to take good care of his sheep.
- God trusted David to be a loyal king.
- God trusted Samuel to anoint the right man when he went to anoint a new king.
- The Israelite army trusted David to kill Goliath.
- David trusted God to keep him safe when he was fighting Goliath.
- David trusted Jonathan even though he was Saul's son.
- David trusted Saul but Saul wanted to kill him. Several times David trusted Saul and Saul tried to kill him again.
- Saul trusted Jonathan to kill David but Jonathan's loyalty was to David.
- David trusted that Jonathan would not set a trap for him with Saul.
- Saul trusted Jonathan's advice about David.
- David trusted Saul when he went back to the palace.
- David trusted his wife, Michal, even though she was Saul's daughter.
- Saul thought he could trust his daughter, Michal, but found out that he could not.
- Jonathan trusted that his dad, Saul, was not trying to kill David.
- David trusted God to protect him from King Saul.
- David and Jonathan trusted each other.
- David showed trust in God by not killing Saul.
- David showed a lack of trust in God by not taking the ark

Materials
miscellaneous props constructed from poster board such as a shepherd's staff, harp, sling shot, crown, sword

of the covenant to Jerusalem.
- David showed trust in his relationship with Jonathan, even after his death, by contacting Mephibosheth.
- David's sin broke down his trust with God.

Suggested discussion questions: When do you think it was the most difficult for David to trust? When do you think it was the most difficult for David to trust God?

Divide students into two teams. Play a relay game to review events in David's life and times that he demonstrated trust. Position both teams at one end of the room. Place the props at the other end of the room. Instruct students to take turns running, grabbing a prop, and telling a life fact or a way that David trusted or did not trust, and then returning to their team. The students can shout out a fact they remember about David or recall a time that David demonstrated or did not demonstrate trust. The team that gets the most facts correct wins.

Step 3

Before class, write the trust quiz from page 62 on a piece of poster board.

Ask the students to take the quiz on the top half of page 62 to see what they think about trust. After the students have answered the questions, have each student record his answers on the poster board. Give each student four mini self-stick notes. Ask them to stick a self-stick note beside each multiple choice answer they chose.

When all the students have answered, have a student tally the results. Discuss each question and each answer. Affirm the students' efforts to be honest and transparent.

Save the poster board so you can study it later. You will learn a lot about the make up of the group of students you will be teaching. By looking at the responses to the quiz, you will be able to project what to emphasize about trust in the next few sessions.

Ask your students to take the quiz again after **Session 4** to see if their views on trust have changed.

Ask the students who prepared the pantomimes to present them now. Guess the various issues of trust in each skit. Talk about ways that Lauren is breaking down the trust between she and her mother and the impact it may have on their relationship. Discuss other action steps John could take as he adjusts to his parents' divorce.

Play the relay game from Step 2 again. This time divide the students into two teams and instruct them to run to the other end of the room, shout an example of their demonstrating trust, and then run back to their team.

Materials
photocopies of page 62, poster board, self-stick notes, pens or pencils

Take It to the Next Level

Give each student a slip of paper. Ask the students to write their answers to this question: What can I do to be more trustworthy? Give students a couple of minutes to write their responses on the paper. They should not write their names. Then ask the students to take about one minute to pray, asking God's help to accomplish what they wrote.

Instruct the students to put their answers in the jar. Mix up the paper slips and ask each student to draw one from the jar. Instruct the students to take about one minute to pray for the person whose slip they drew.

Materials

slips of paper, pens or pencils, large empty jar such as a quart Mason or mayonnaise jar

Trust Quiz

1. I trust other people like
    a. a cat trusts a dog.
    b. a newborn baby trusts her mom.
    c. a detective trusts a criminal.

2. I think trust really means
    a. making sure no one can take advantage of me.
    b. being confident in someone's loyalty to me.
    c. relying on someone else.

3. What does trust look like?
    a. praying to God.
    b. talking to my dad about a problem at school.
    c. lending my favorite sweatshirt to my best friend.

4. I want to improve my ability to trust by
    a. trusting someone who has hurt me.
    b. building a better relationship with God.
    c. being more trustworthy.

Case Studies

One of the rules at Lauren's house is to come straight home from school. Lauren is usually home after school for about an hour before her mom gets home from work. One day last week, Jessica asked Lauren to come home with her so she could show Lauren her new keyboard. Lauren really wanted to see the keyboard because she has been wanting one also. So she went with Jessica. She knew she had enough time to go to Jessica's house and be home before her mom got home from work. Her mom would never know.

Aaron's parents talked to him over the weekend about a big change in his family. His parents were going to get a divorce. Not only were they not going to be together in one house anymore, but they wanted him to decided who he wanted to live with. Everything in his life was going to be different. He was really mad at both his mom and his dad. He didn't know what to do. When he got to church on Sunday morning he told his Sunday school teacher and class. They prayed for him. When he was leaving class he told his teacher that he felt a little better.

Session 2

Trusting Comrades

Scripture: 1 Samuel 18:1-4; 19:1-7; 20; 23:7, 8, 13, 14, 16-18; 31:1-3; 2 Samuel 9

Know how to have trusting relationships.
Feel convicted to build trusting relationships.
Work on building trust in relationships.

Get Into the Game

Guide your students to participate in a trust experiment. Set up an obstacle course using chairs, tables, or other large objects. in the class area or hallway. Divide the students into pairs. Give each pair a blindfold or bandanna. In each pair, one person is the leader and one the follower. The follower is blindfolded. Instruct the leaders to talk their blindfolded followers through the obstacle course. They should not touch the follower unless he gets into trouble and they need to save him. Have all the pairs do this trust walk simultaneously. Each follower will have to listen closely for his leader's voice. Reinforce to the leaders the importance of being trustworthy and not playing tricks on their followers. Allow enough time for the pairs to switch roles.

Encourage the students to tell about their experiences.

Suggested discussion questions: Followers, why was it hard to trust your leader? Leaders, what was difficult about leading your partner, knowing that he trusted you? How did you demonstrate trust?

Materials
chairs, tables, blindfolds or bandannas

Step 1

Activity #1

Before the session, write these Scripture references on index cards: 1 Samuel 18:1-4; 1 Samuel 19:1-7; 1 Samuel 20; 1 Samuel 23:7, 8, 13, 14, 16-18; 1 Samuel 31:1-3; 2 Samuel 9.

Divide the students into six groups. Give each group an index card with a Scripture reference on it. Instruct the students to read the Scripture. Each Scripture tells about an event in the relationship between Jonathan and David.

Materials
miscellaneous props, corrugated cardboard, poster board, markers, index cards

Tell the students they are to prepare a skit retelling the event in a modern allegory. Here are a couple of examples.

1. 1 Samuel 18:1-4. Two preteens are such good friends that they promise to always be best friends. To show how serious they are about their friendship, they trade something that is very valuable to them.

2. 1 Samuel 31:1-3. A preteen's friend dies and she talks about how upset she is, how much she will miss her friend, and what good friends they were.

Encourage the students to use the props you have provided.

A brief summary of David and Jonathan's friendship follows to help you focus your students' attention.

Jonathan became friends with David. Jonathan made a covenant with David. He gave David his robe, tunic, sword, bow, and belt. David probably gave Jonathan the same things to show his friendship to Jonathan. A covenant relationship, like the one David and Jonathan established, was a relationship with God at its center. Jonathan's loyalty to David was greater than his loyalty to his family. Even after Jonathan realized David, not he, would succeed Saul on the throne, he still remained David's committed friend.

Jonathan's father, King Saul, told him to kill David. Instead of carrying out the task, Jonathan warned David. And he talked to his father on David's behalf, telling him how loyal David was. Jonathan convinced his father not to kill David at that time. Jonathan went to David and brought him back to Saul's house.

But Saul soon felt threatened by David's battle victories again and ordered to have David killed. Jonathan again went to his father and defended David. Saul was so mad he tried to kill Jonathan. Jonathan went back to David to warn him.

Saul continued to hunt for David so that he could kill him. Jonathan came to David during this time to encourage him. He told him Saul would not kill him and that David would become king. Jonathan affirmed his loyalty to David once again.

Jonathan was killed in a battle against the Philistines, Israel's greatest threat at the time. David was very upset about losing his best friend.

After David was king, he wanted to show kindness to Jonathan's family. He discovered that Jonathan had a son named Mephibosheth, who had a physical disability. David provided for Mephibosheth the rest of his life as if he were David's own son.

Activity #2

Give each student twenty marshmallows. Let each build a marshmallow tower. The towers could be pyramid style or one marshmallow on top of another.

Materials
large marshmallows, toothpicks

In order to add a marshmallow to their towers, each student must state something about how to build a trusting relationship. For example, be trustworthy yourself; put God at the center of the relationship; be honest; base the relationship on godly principles; be loyal.

Your students will want to rush through their responses so they can concentrate on building their towers. Linger on each response, however, so that you can discuss trust thoroughly.

Once the students have tried to build the tallest marshmallow towers, give them twenty toothpicks. Instruct the students to use the toothpicks between each marshmallow as they build a new tower. Ask students about trust again as they build their towers. The students will realize their towers are much more stable and can be built taller with the toothpicks inserted in the marshmallows. Use this as an illustration of the importance of trust in relationships. Trust makes relationships more stable. Relationships can be built deeper and are more long lasting when they are built around trust.

Suggested discussion questions: How do you build trust in a relationship? What is trust? Why is trust important to a relationship?

(Note: As a variation on this activity, the students could work in pairs to build the towers. This will test their ability to trust each other.)

Activity #3

Ask students to make a list on the overhead transparency of who they trust and why. Encourage students to think of people who are close to them, such as parents, grandparents, school friends, teachers, coaches. Encourage students to also think of people such as police officers, neighbors, doctors, or store clerks.

Talk about specific ways trust is demonstrated in the different relationships with these people. For example, we trust police officers to uphold the law; we trust parents to take care of us; we trust our friends to be loyal to us. Should issues of broken trust come up in your conversation, discuss them briefly and then move on. Broken trust will be discussed extensively in **Session 3.**

Suggested discussion questions: Why do you trust the people who you do? How do you build trust in a relationship? Why is trust important in a relationship?

Materials
overhead projector, overhead transparency, overhead pens

Step 2

Ask students who prepared skits retelling David and Jonathan's friendship in a modern-day setting to present them now. Talk about each event as the students present them. Review the details from Scripture. A summary of the Scripture is included with Activity #1. Direct the students' discussion to focus on ways Jonathan and David demonstrated trust in each other.

Suggested discussion questions: When did David trust Jonathan? When did Jonathan trust David? When may it have been difficult for David to have trusted Jonathan?

Step 3

Ask students to shout the names of people they trust (parents, friends, teachers, coaches, doctors, neighbors). Ask, "Why do you trust them?" The students who made the overhead transparency can show it now.

Discuss with the students the importance of trust in a relationship. Talk about specific ways trust is demonstrated in various relationships. As you discuss people your students trust, they may mention times when trust has been broken. Steer the conversation away from broken trust or problems with trusting people. This will be discussed in **Session 3.** Simply acknowledge that trust does break down sometimes.

Use the following information to help guide your discussion.

Parents—We trust our parents to love us, make right decisions for us, have our best interests in mind. Trusting our parents comes very naturally to us because we do so from the time we are born.

Friends—We trust our friends to be loyal, honest, kind, considerate. The more we get to know our friends, the more we trust them. It takes time and energy to develop trust in our friendships.

Teachers, coaches, and other adult authority figures—Preteens develop trust in adults based on the various roles they play in their lives. If the preteens know the adults care about them, then they will trust them.

Ask the students who built the marshmallow towers to demonstrate how much sturdier their towers were when they used the toothpicks than when they did not. Guide those students to discuss how that symbolizes trust in a relationship.

Have the students divide into pairs. Guide the students to try the trust walk from Get Into the Game again. This time, instead of using blindfolds, have the follower simply close his eyes as the leader guides him around the room. The follower still must trust the leader to guide him carefully. But this time the leader must trust the follower to keep his eyes closed.

Take It to the Next Level

Distribute photocopies of page 68 and pens or pencils. Instruct the students to read the situations. They should be able to identify trust in the relationships. Allow students to do most of the discussing. Guide their conversation as necessary.

Materials
photocopies of page 68, pens or pencils

How trustworthy am I?

- I cut a deal with my dad. He let me stay up late to watch the NBA finals. I told him that I would help him clean out the garage over the weekend without complaining. But I didn't know Ben was going to ask me to an overnight camping trip. I can't believe Dad is going to make me stay home and work on Saturday. He knows what good friends Ben and I are.

- Courtney and I have been friends since we were in kindergarten. She has started acting really weird lately. She wants to hang around with some different kids. They do some things that I think are wrong. The other day she was making fun of one of our friends in the cafeteria. I just don't understand. I'm going to have to talk to her about it. I just want to know if she is OK.

- I told Mrs. Sanwald that I forgot my homework and that I would bring it the next day. It was great. She didn't even know that I hadn't done it. I could go home, do it that night, and turn it in the next day. I would still get a good grade even though it was late. Boy, did I pull one over on her!

Write Your Own
Tell about a time that you have or have not been trustworthy.

_____
_____
_____
_____
_____
_____
_____
_____

Session 3

You're Breaking Up . . .

Scripture: 1 Samuel 16; 17; 18:1-5, 10, 11, 17-30; 19:1-7, 9-24; 20; 23:7-18; 24:1-22; 26:1-25; 2 Samuel 6:6, 7; 22

Know what to do when a relationship's trust is broken.
Feel convicted to build trusting relationships.
Work on rebuilding trust in a relationship.

Get Into the Game

Before class, talk to one student about being a decoy in a game of telephone. Tell him how the game is played. Then tell him you want him to change the sentence in the second round to something drastically different from the sentence you start. Tell him the sentence you will use and come up with a sentence for him to use.

Instruct the students to play a game of old-fashioned "telephone." Tell the students to sit on the floor in a circle. You sit directly across from the student you talked to before class. You will whisper a sentence in the ear of the student to your right. That student is to whisper the sentence in the next student's ear. Repeat until the sentence has been whispered all the way around the circle. The last student is to say the sentence aloud. Then you say the sentence you started with. The sentences may or may not match exactly. Each person can only whisper the sentence once. The listener must repeat to the next person what she thought she heard. Play one round using a sentence such as, "My favorite time of year is winter because there is snow on the ground."

Play a second round using the student you talked to before class. When the last student says the sentence aloud, the students will realize the sentences are drastically different. Let the students interact for a minute without giving away your secret.

Then tell the students that the decoy student changed the sentence halfway around the circle. Let the students react. Focus the conversation on the fact that the students' trust was broken. The students trusted the student to their left to whisper the sentence accurately.

Suggested discussion questions: How did you demonstrate

trust as you played the telephone game? How did you feel when you found out the student changed the sentence? If we were to play telephone again, would you trust that student to play the game correctly? Would you give him a second chance? Why or why not?

Step 1

Activity #1

Instruct a group of students to create a skit in which they interview David about trust, what he did when he could not trust someone, and how he trusted someone after his trust in them had been broken. The students will need to review the main events in David's life from **Session 1.** Help them focus on the times that David demonstrated trust—in Saul (1 Samuel 16:14-23; 18:5, 17-30; 19:7; 24:1-22), in Jonathan (1 Samuel 18:1-4; 19:1-6; 20; 23:16-18), and in God (1 Samuel 16:1-13; 17; 24:1-22; 26:7-25; 2 Samuel 22). They also need to identify times that David's trust was broken—Saul tried to kill him several times (1 Samuel 18:10, 11; 19:1-3, 9-24; 20:35-42; 23:7-15; 26:1-6); God killed Uzzah for touching the ark (2 Samuel 6:6, 7). And they need to identify what David did to trust again.

Once students have recalled these historical events from David's life, guide students to develop the dialogue for an interview with David. Each student should have a role in the skit: David, the interviewer, the cameraman, the producer, etc. The interviewer should ask questions to reveal the events in David's life when he could not trust someone and how he trusted someone after his trust in that person had been broken. The interviewer should also ask feeling questions—How did you feel when . . . ?

Sample interview questions: Why did you continue to trust Saul? Why didn't you kill Saul? How did you feel when you went back to Saul after he had tried to kill you? How did you demonstrate trust in God? Why was it easy to trust Jonathan? How did you feel when Saul died? How did you feel when Jonathan was killed?

Activity #2

Before the session, break the terra cotta flower pot into several large pieces. Glue the pot back together with hot glue or a strong multipurpose glue.

Discuss with the students times that their trust has been broken. Encourage each student to share a particular instance of broken trust. Ask him questions to find out what type of relationship it was (parent, friend, coach), what happened to break the trust, and what the student did after the trust was broken.

Materials
miscellaneous props

Materials
10" or larger terra cotta flower pot, hot glue and gun or strong multipurpose glue, permanent markers

Discuss positive action steps to take and actions that may be incorrect. Encourage the students in their attempts to trust again—whether it is the same person or in another relationship.

Write a summary phrase on each piece of the broken terra cotta pot. For example, parent lied, coach was unfair, friend betrayed, teacher didn't follow through, parent left. Do not write on the rim of the flower pot.

Your students may share some very painful stories during this time. Be sensitive to their emotions. Should a student share a circumstance in which his trust was broken through abuse, be sure to talk with him privately. Take necessary legal steps as well (see page 74).

Suggested discussion questions: Have you ever trusted someone and then found out that you couldn't trust him? What did you do? What are some circumstances when you should not trust that person again? What can you do to rebuild trust?

Activity #3

Instruct students to read each case study on page 75. Focus their conversation on action steps each student could take in his circumstance of broken trust.

Use the following information to help guide your discussion.

Michael may feel as if he can't trust his mom because he thought his dad was coming back. He may feel as if he can't trust his dad because his dad left and is now getting a divorce. Michael could do several things: pray, talk to someone to help him understand, forgive his dad for leaving, tell his mom and dad how he feels, decide to trust his mom and dad again, love his mom and dad even more because they are hurting too.

Jessica should not continue to trust the teenage boy next door. Jessica needs to tell her parents what is happening. No matter how embarrassing it may be, Jessica is in danger and the boy needs to be stopped. Discuss with your students other times that broken trust should not be rebuilt. Carefully listen to see if a student shares an abusive circumstance and take the necessary actions.

Materials
photocopies of page 75

Step 2

Have students who created a skit interviewing David present it now. Following their presentation, focus the students' attention on times in David's life when he could not trust someone. Use the following information to guide your discussion.

David demonstrated his trust in King Saul several times. Initially he trusted Saul enough to move into his home. David became acquainted with Saul when he played his harp for the king. David eventually achieved a high rank as an officer in Saul's army. And David married one of King Saul's daughters, Michal. He became a member of the family.

Yet Saul could not be trusted. He tried to kill David several times. He was jealous of David's victories in battle and was concerned that David was more popular than he was.

Even after several murder attempts, David showed some level of trust in King Saul. Some of this trust may have been as a result of David's respect for Saul as God's anointed king. David carefully trusted Saul after he knew Saul was capable of killing him.

Unlike Saul, David knew he could trust Jonathan. Jonathan never gave him any reason not to trust him. Jonathan and David had committed their relationship to God, saying they would be godly friends. So Jonathan was very loyal to David. Even when his own father was trying to kill David, Jonathan warned David, talked to King Saul on David's behalf, and tried to protect David.

David also shows trust in God. David must have been a godly man because God chose him as the next king of Israel. David demonstrated his trust in God several times in his life. He trusted that God would take care of him before Goliath and the Philistines. He trusted that he would survive King Saul's attacks.

David also demonstrated mistrust in God. When David had ordered a group of men to bring the Ark of the Covenant back to Jerusalem, one man handled the ark improperly. God killed him. David decided not to bring the ark to Jerusalem at that time. He didn't understand God's actions. He thought he could not trust God.

Suggested discussion questions: How do you think David felt when he realized he could not trust King Saul? Why must it have been easy for David to have a trusting relationship with Jonathan? How did David show he trusted God? What can you learn from David's relationship with King Saul? With Jonathan? With God?

Step 3

Before class, make several photocopies of the cards shown on page 75. Cut the cards apart. Each student will need at least one crown card and one arrow card. Guide students to recognize who their Jonathan is—someone they can always trust. Next encourage the students to think of someone they would identify as a King Saul—someone they cannot always trust. Ask the students to write the name of their Jonathan on an arrow card and the name of their King Saul on a crown card.

Materials
photocopies of page 75 cut apart

Next ask the students why they trust their Jonathan. Invite them to write their responses on the arrow card. Guide the discussion as necessary to reinforce that we trust people because they love us, take care of us, are loyal to us, tell us the truth, and are kind to us.

Celebrate trustworthiness. Lead a short prayer time with your students praising God for these trustworthy Jonathans. Invite the students to thank God and praise Him for each of their Jonathans by name.

Ask the students why they believe their King Sauls are not always trustworthy. Encourage the students to write their responses on their crown cards. As the students answer, make a master list on a piece of poster board or on a chalkboard. Ask the students what actions they have taken when their King Sauls have not been trustworthy. Add these student answers to the master list.

Have the students who studied the case studies report now. They should read the case studies and discuss the action steps they developed. Add these action steps to your master list.

Review by talking through the three areas on your master list—why people are not trustworthy, actions taken when people are not trustworthy, and actions to take when people are not trustworthy.

Take It to the Next Level

Ask the students to write the appropriate action steps for trusting their King Sauls on their crown cards. Encourage them to pick one or two actions steps from your master list. Talk about the importance of carrying out the action steps in the next one or two weeks.

Guide the students to take the broken flower pot from the activity center and write this sentence around the rim of the pot: When trust is broken, we can trust again. You could also add the verse, Romans 8:37. Line the pot with heavy plastic and help the students plant a house plant in the pot. Leave the potted plant in your classroom or meeting area to remind the students that some relationships can live on when trust is broken if we take the appropriate actions steps.

Students could also pot their own small plants in individual pots to take home. Have them write the sentence on their small pot before transplanting a plant.

What to Do if You Suspect Abuse

You can obtain your state's child abuse laws from the Department of Child Welfare, the district attorney's office, or a local law enforcement agency. Check your local phone book for addresses and telephone numbers.

Definitions of abuse and neglect vary from state to state. Basically, child abuse is a misuse of an adult's power and authority over a child under eighteen that leads to damage and has no reasonable explanation. In general, abuse and neglect refer to specific acts of commission or omission that cause harm to a child's physical, mental, or emotional development. Forms of abuse are usually identified as physical abuse, emotional abuse, neglect, and sexual abuse or exploitation.

If a student discloses that he has been abused, you should react calmly. Your first reaction will influence how he will feel about himself as a result of telling you.

• **Listen** calmly and carefully. Don't put words in his mouth or ask leading questions.

• **Believe** the student. It isn't your responsibility to determine whether or not he is telling the truth.

• **Protect** the student's privacy. Talk to her alone. Assure her that you will see she gets help.

• **Affirm** the student's feelings. Assure him that what happened was not his fault, and praise him for his courage and honesty.

Report the disclosure to a church staff person and follow up to make sure it is reported to the authorities. It is very important to contact the child protection authorities as soon as possible. Too much questioning by untrained adults can be more detrimental than helpful. Do not confront the accused until the victim's safety is insured.

Taking Action Case Studies

Read each case study and think of what action can be taken. Discuss the actions with your class.

Michael didn't understand when his dad moved into an apartment six months ago. His mom said Michael's dad needed to do some thinking and wanted to be by himself. Now Michael's mom says they are getting a divorce. There is so much that Michael doesn't understand. Doesn't his dad love them anymore? Why wouldn't he want to live with them? Michael doesn't know how to feel. He's mad at his mom and his dad. He's hurt. He's confused.

Jessica is really confused by the teenage boy who lives next door to her. He tried to touch her in places that he shouldn't have been touching. He's tried it before too. She really likes him because he is cute. Even though he's fifteen, he always pays attention to her. Now she doesn't know what to do. He is so nice to her. When he touches her like that, she always runs in her house; it scares her. But then the next time she sees him, he acts as if nothing happened.

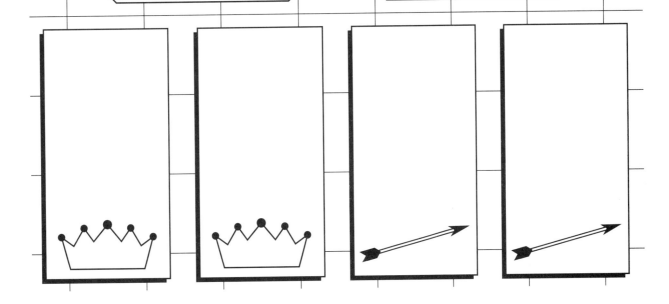

Session 4

Trust Trek With God

Scripture: 1 Samuel 16:1-13; 17; 23:7-14; 24:1-10; 2 Samuel 2:1-4; 6:1-12; 7:18, 19, 22, 28; 11:1-17, 26, 27; Psalm 51:1, 2, 10-12; Acts 13:22

Know how to trust God.
Feel convicted to build trusting relationships.
Work on building a trusting relationship with God.

Get Into the Game

Before the session, cut a 4" circle in the lid of six shoe boxes. Place one of these items in each shoe box: water-soaked crackers in a bowl; fake fur cut to fit the bottom of the box; cold pudding in a bowl; peeled grapes in a bowl; styrofoam packing peanuts; crumpled sheets of sandpaper.

Line up the prepared shoe boxes on a table. Tell students you want them to identify what is in each shoe box, but they must identify it by touch. Give students paper and pencils. Instruct them to write down numbers one through six. Guide the students to put one hand in a box, feel what is inside, and write down what they think it is on the piece of paper. Continue from box to box.

When all the students have guessed what is in each box, reveal the contents of each box. Discuss with the students how they had to trust you by putting their hands in the shoe boxes. They also had to trust in something they could not see. Explain that this is very much like trusting God. We must trust other people and trust things we cannot see.

Suggested discussion questions: How did you have to trust me? How did you demonstrate trust in something you could not see? How do you demonstrate trust in God?

Materials
six shoe boxes with lids, water-soaked crackers in a bowl, fake fur, cold pudding in a bowl, peeled grapes in a bowl, styrofoam packing peanuts, sheets of sandpaper, pens or pencils, paper, scissors

Step 1
Activity #1

Before the session, make a masking-tape road on the floor of your classroom or meeting area. Wind the road around the room. Write each set of Scriptures listed below in bold type on an index card.

Materials
masking tape, construction paper, markers, pencils, plastic cups, 12" rulers, scissors

Guide students to make road signs that represent the various times David trusted God or did not trust God throughout his life. They can draw a picture or write a short summary. They can use the construction paper and markers. They could cut the construction paper into a road sign shape. Tape the completed signs on the end of a ruler. Cut a slit in the bottom of the plastic cup wide enough for the ruler to slide through. Stand each sign in an upside-down plastic cup along the masking-tape road in chronological order. If you do not want students to complete all eight Scripture passages, prepare some of them yourself before class.

A summary of each Scripture passage follows.

1. 1 Samuel 16:1-13; Acts 13:22. David was anointed to succeed Saul as king of Israel. God trusted David to lead His people. He knew David had the right kind of heart.

2. 1 Samuel 17. David killed Goliath. David trusted God to deliver him from Goliath (verse 37).

3. 1 Samuel 23:7-14. God warned David of Saul's intentions to kill him. David trusted God to protect him from Saul.

4. 1 Samuel 24:1-10. David had a chance to kill Saul but chose not to. David demonstrated his respect for God and the man He chose as king.

5. 2 Samuel 2:1-4. David was anointed king after Saul's death. David trusted that what God said through Samuel was true. And he did become king.

6. 2 Samuel 6:1-12. David was afraid to bring the Ark of the Covenant to Jerusalem because God killed Uzzah for touching the ark. It was against Hebrew law to touch the ark (Numbers 4:5-15). Uzzah's death was partially David's fault because the men were not Levites and were not moving the ark properly. They were moving it on a cart instead of on poles on Levites' shoulders. David neglected one of God's laws and a man died. David did bring the ark to Jerusalem but he ordered it to be brought properly (1 Chronicles 15:11-15). David eventually trusted that God would not kill him or strike down his kingdom.

7. 2 Samuel 7:18, 19, 22, 28. David prayed to God. David recognized the importance of trusting God and relying on Him.

8. 2 Samuel 11:1-17, 26, 27; Psalm 51:1, 2, 10-12. David committed adultery with Bathsheba and then had her husband killed so that he could marry her. God was very displeased with David's sins. David broke the trust between himself and God. David was sorry for what he had done and prayed for forgiveness (Psalms 51). He wanted to have a trusting relationship with God again.

Activity #2

Before the session, prepare a sample trust trek journal.

Guide students to make trust trek journals. They will decorate the outside of a binder folder with markers and construction paper. Have them create a title for their journals. For example, *Trust Trek Journal, My Journey With God, My Trust Trek With God.* Instruct students to put a Scripture on their journals. For example: Proverbs 3:5, 6; Psalm 25:4, 5; Isaiah 8:17. Students will put at least twenty-five photocopies of page 82 in their journals.

How to use the journals will be explained in **Take It to the Next Level.** However, as the students work on constructing their journals, you could discuss the various sections of the journal page.

Materials
photocopies of page 82 on several colors of paper, binder folder (various colors), markers, construction paper, glue, pencils

Activity #3

Instruct students to think of times they have trusted God. Give each student an opportunity to share about the time. Guide the students to make a road sign similar to the ones constructed in Activity #1. Cut a road sign shape from construction paper. Use any shape but a stop sign. Instruct the students to write or draw about the times they trusted God.

Instruct students to tell about times they did not trust God. They should construct stop signs for these times. Instruct the students to cut stop signs from red construction paper and write or draw about the times they did not trust God.

Tape the completed signs on the end of a ruler. Cut a slit in the bottom of the plastic cup wide enough for the ruler to slide through. Stand each sign in an upside-down plastic cup. These signs will be added to the masking tape road in Step 3.

Materials
red construction paper, markers, pencils, plastic cups, 12" rulers, scissors

Step 2

Discuss the various times David trusted God or did not trust God throughout his life. Students who completed Activity #1 can walk the other students along their masking-tape road. Guide them to review each sign along the road. They need to emphasize whether the sign represents a time that David trusted God or did not trust God.

Use the following information to focus the students' attention on trusting God.

When David was anointed to succeed Saul as king of Israel, God demonstrated trust in David. David was probably already a godly man. He probably developed a trusting relationship with God during the many hours he was alone tending his father's sheep. He may have even written songs of worship to God like he did when he wrote some of the Psalms. God trusted David to lead His people as king. He knew David had the right kind of heart.

When David killed Goliath, David trusted God to deliver him from Goliath. Even though Goliath was much larger and stronger than David, David knew he had God on his side. Why would God let David die if he had been anointed as the next king?

God warned David when King Saul wanted to kill him. David trusted God to protect him from Saul. And God protected David several times. King Saul would have killed David if it wasn't for God.

David also had chances to kill Saul but chose not to. David knew that Saul was God's anointed to be king for that time. David demonstrated his respect for God.

David was anointed king after Saul's death. David trusted that what God said through Samuel was true. And he did become king.

David was afraid to bring the Ark of the Covenant to Jerusalem because God killed Uzzah for touching the ark. David neglected one of God's laws and a man died. David demonstrated that he was afraid of what God may have done. David was not sure that he trusted God.

David did bring the ark to Jerusalem but he ordered it be brought properly, according to God's laws for moving the ark. David eventually trusted that God would not kill him or strike down his kingdom.

David committed adultery with Bathsheba and then had her husband killed so he could marry her. God was very displeased with David's sins. David broke the trust between he and God. David was very sorry for what he had done and prayed for forgiveness. He wanted to have a trusting relationship with God again.

David prayed to God many times. We have many of his prayers recorded in the Psalms. David recognized the importance of trusting God and relying on Him.

Give each student a photocopy of page 82. Invite the preteens to fill out the journal page as if they were David. Here are some suggestions for how the sentences could be filled in.

I trusted God when . . .
. . . I went to live with King Saul.
. . . I fought Goliath.
. . . I cut off King Saul's robe.
. . . I prayed for forgiveness for my sins.
. . . I became king.
. . . I decided to bring the Ark of the Covenant to Jerusalem.

I didn't rely on God when . . .
. . . I committed adultery with Bathsheba.
. . . I had Uriah killed.
. . . I chose not to bring the Ark of the Covenant to Jerusalem.

Dear God,
I know that You love me and want me to love and trust You. Please be patient with me. The most important thing in my life is to serve You.

Love,
David

What God might say to me:
You are trying very hard. You demonstrate trust in me almost every day. Keep working on being a godly man. I love you too.

Step 3

Guide students who completed Activity #3 to add their road signs to the masking-tape road in the classroom or meeting area. They may want to put all of the road signs about David's life on one side of the road and their road signs on the other side of the road. Intersperse the stop signs evenly along the road with the times that the students did not trust God.

Students who completed Activity #3 should walk the other students along the masking-tape road and stop at each road sign. Whoever made the sign should tell about the time he or she demonstrated trust in God.

When the students come to a stop sign, ask the students to stop and sit down. Guide the students to discuss why this is an example of not trusting God. Have a student or pair of students role-play a way to demonstrate trust in God in this situation or a similar one. Move on to the next sign when you think the discussion has been thorough enough.

Discuss how God knows we trust Him. Our actions must show our faith in Him.

Take It to the Next Level

Have students who completed Activity #2 show and talk about their trust trek journals. Guide other students to make their own journals at this time if they have not done so. Talk about samples of what to write in each section. Use David's journal entry from Step 2 as an example. The students can complete a page for a day or for a week. Talk about where to keep the journals, when to write in the journals, and the importance of thinking about how we demonstrate trust in God.

Instruct the students to fill out their first journal page in this class time. Give the students about ten minutes to accomplish this. Encourage the students to take their journal, Bible, and pen to any place in the classroom or meeting area. Some may want to sit on the floor, lay on the floor, or sit at a table. Encourage them to do what they feel comfortable doing in order to write in their journals. Tell the students to write in each section of the journal page, and then spend a few minutes praying and reading their Bibles.

End the class with a group prayer time. Focus on praying for God's direction as the students try to trust Him more.

Review Note

Before the session, make photocopies of the trust quiz on page 62. Instruct the students to take the quiz again. Compare their answers to how they answered in **Session 1.** You may want to complete the self-stick note activity from Step 3 of **Session 1** for further review.

My Trust Trek With God

Date _____

I trusted God when . . .
_____
_____
_____
_____
_____
_____
_____

I didn't rely on God when . . .
_____
_____
_____
_____
_____
_____
_____
_____
_____

Dear God,
_____
_____
_____
_____
_____
_____
_____
_____
_____
_____
_____
_____
_____
_____
_____
_____
_____

Love, _____

What God might say to me:

"Trust in the LORD with all your heart and lean not on your own understanding; in all your ways acknowledge him, and he will make your paths straight" (Proverbs 3:5, 6).

_____
_____
_____
_____
_____
_____
_____

Bridge the Gap

Trust Trek Trip

Plan a trust experience for the entire family as the last session of this unit. The event is designed so that family members of all ages will build trust in their family unit.

Invitations

Students can make invitations to the Trust Trek Trip out of colorful paper and markers. Guide the students to make an invitation for each family member they are inviting. You may want to include an R.S.V.P. to help in your planning.

Trust Reports

Prior to this session, students could prepare a short presentation telling about trust. These presentations could be as simple as a student talking about what he learned during a particular session. Or a group of students could present one of the activities they completed for a session.

Here are some ideas.

Unit Projects. Invite any students who completed a unit project to share it with the group. Instruct them to explain what they did and what they learned about trust.

Session 1. Have the students display the everyday things we trust that they constructed from *Play-Doh* in Activity #2 (pages

57 and 58). These items could be placed on an eight-foot table somewhere in your meeting area. At an appropriate time, invite the students to talk about their creations.

Session 2. Instruct families to build the marshmallow towers from Activity #2 (pages 64 and 65). Give each family twenty marshmallows. Tell them to build one marshmallow tower together. The towers could be pyramid style or one marshmallow on top of another. Once the families have tried to build a tower using all of the marshmallows, give them twenty toothpicks. Instruct the families to use the toothpicks in-between each marshmallow as they build a tower. Instruct each student to tell his or her family how this is an illustration of trust in a relationship. Ask families to answer this question: How do we build trust in our family?

Session 3. Display the flower pot or pots that were completed at the end of this session. Encourage a student to talk about how we can trust again after trust has been broken. Read Romans 8:37. Talk about how some relationships can live on when trust is broken if we take the appropriate actions steps. Instruct students to tell what some of those actions steps might be.

Session 4. Include a short devotion from David's life during the Trust Trek Trip. Talk about the times that David trusted or did not trust King Saul. Talk about the trusting relationship David and Jonathan had. Talk about times that David demonstrated trust in God.

Trust Experiences

Allow time for the families to develop trust in their family unit. Guide them to experience the trust experiments from the four trust sessions. You may want to spread these experiences throughout the Trust Trek Trip.

Trust Circle. Guide the families to participate in a trust experiment as a family. Designate one student as *It*. The other family members will stand in a circle shoulder to shoulder facing in. *It* stands in the center of his family's circle and crosses his arms across his chest.

It stiffens his body and falls backwards. His family catches him around the arms and shoulders and passes him to other family members while his feet remain on the floor. Continue passing *It* around the circle several more times. This works best if *It* keeps his feet together and near the center of the circle. (Note: Two or more families may need to do this activity together if some families are few in number.)

Trust Walk. Set up an obstacle course using chairs, tables, or other large objects in the meeting area or hallway. Depending on how many families you have participating, you may want to set up two or more obstacles courses. Divide each family into pairs. If you have an odd number, one family member can participate twice. Give each pair a blindfold (bandannas work well). In each pair, one person is the leader and one the follower. The follower is blindfolded. Instruct the leaders to talk their blindfolded followers through the obstacle course. They should not touch the follower unless he gets into trouble and they need to save him. Have all the family pairs do this trust walk simultaneously. Each follower will have to listen closely for his leader's voice. Reinforce to the leaders the importance of being trustworthy and not playing tricks on their followers. Allow enough time for the pairs to switch roles.

Trust Telephone. Before this session, talk to one person about being a decoy in a game of telephone. Tell him how the game is played. Then tell him you want him to change the sentence in the second round to something drastically different from the sentence you start. Tell him the sentence you will use and come up with a sentence for him to use.

Instruct the families to play a game of old-fashioned "telephone." Have families sit on the floor in a circle. You may want to divide the families into several circles, depending on how many people are participating. You sit directly across from the person you talked to before the session. You will whisper a sentence in the ear of the person to your right. That person is to whisper the sentence in the next person's ear. Repeat until the sentence has been whispered all the way around the circle. The last person is to say the sentence aloud. Then you say the sentence you started with. The sentences may or may not match exactly. Each person can only whisper the sentence once. The listener must repeat to the next person what she thought she heard. Play one round using a sentence such as, "My favorite time of year is winter because snow's on the ground."

Play a second round using the person you talked to before this session. When the last person says the sentence aloud, the participants will realize the sentences are drastically different. Let the participants interact for a minute without giving your secret away.

Then tell the participants that the decoy person changed the sentence halfway around the circle. Let the participants react. Focus the conversation on the fact that the trust was broken.

Trust Boxes. Use the shoe boxes you prepared for Get Into the Game in **Session 4** (see page 76). Line up the prepared shoe boxes on a table. Tell the family members you want them to identify what is in each shoe box. But they must identify it by their touch. They must demonstrate trust in you. Distribute paper and pencils. Instruct everyone to write numbers one through six on their papers. Guide the participants to put their hands in a box, feel what is inside, and write down what they think it is on the piece of paper. Continue from box to box.

When all the participants have had a chance to guess what is in each box, reveal the contents of each box. Encourage a student to explain how this is like trusting God.

Trust Cookies

Before the session, make the cookie dough. The recipe makes five dozen 2" inch cookies. Allow two cookies for each family member. Divide each batch into five mixing bowls. Put the extra ingredients in bowls in plain view of everyone.

During the trust trek session, instruct each student to make cookies for his family. He is to add any of the extra ingredients to his batch and form the cookies on a cookie sheet. The student can choose whatever ingredients he thinks his family will enjoy. The family must trust that he will make a batch of good cookies. Help students as necessary.

Cookie Recipe
2 1/4 cups all-purpose flour
1 teaspoon baking soda
1 teaspoon salt
1 cup butter, softened
3/4 cup sugar
3/4 firmly packed brown sugar
1 teaspoon vanilla extract
2 eggs

Preheat oven to 375° F. In a small bowl, combine flour, baking soda, and salt; set aside. In a large bowl, combine butter, sugar, brown sugar, and vanilla extract; beat until creamy. Beat in eggs. Gradually add flour mixture. Drop by teaspoons onto ungreased cookie sheets. Bake at 375°F. 9-11 minutes. Yields about 5 dozen 2" cookies.

Additional ingredients for students to add:
chocolate chips
butterscotch chips
peanut butter chips
chopped nuts
colored sprinkles
Heath brickle
M&M's
raisins
any grated candy bar
grated carrots
pepperoni
apple slices

Go to Extremes

A Prayer Walk

This service project is designed to help students discuss what they have learned about trust. It is also designed to emphasize prayer. The prayer walk is an event involving worship and prayer as a large group, followed by stations centered on specific focuses.

Help your students plan a prayer walk event for another group. Guide the students as they take on the responsibility to plan and implement this event. Encourage their creativity. Help the students divide the responsibilities among themselves.

The students could plan the event for other children their own age. Maybe the students will want to invite the preteen youth groups in your area. Your students could invite your high school youth group or your entire congregation.

Begin the event with a large gathering. The students can plan a fifteen- to twenty-minute presentation to begin the event. Instruct one student to talk about the event: why you have prepared this event, what will happen, how the people will participate. Include some singing during this time. Encourage the students to pick out songs that talk about God's faithfulness and reasons that we can trust Him. "My Trust is in the Name of the Lord," (Integrity's Hosanna! Music) would be a good song to use during this time. This also may be a good time to have a devotion about David and his relationship with God. Have a student prepare a devotional using some of the information shared during this unit.

After this gathering, everyone will be divided into groups and travel from station to station every seven to ten minutes. These stations can be set up in your meeting area. Or they could be in various places in your church building. One station would give directions to the next station if you choose to have your stations all over the building.

Instruct students to plan the various prayer activities at each station. Two students should guide each station. These students would stay at the station as participants move from station to station. Have students make signs on pieces of poster board to hang over each station.

Station 1. Pray for God's direction for your life.

Before the session, guide students to prepare stories from David's life for this station. Have students make several photocopies of the arrow card from page 75 on sturdy paper and cut them out. Each participant will need one card. Gather pens and pencils for this station.

During the event, have the students tell about times that God directed David's life: anointing him as king, going to live in Saul's household. Then participants will write a way that God is directing their lives or a way that they desire direction on the card. Participants can share what they write if they want to. Students at this station will ask participants to pray aloud for God to work in the life of the person to their right. The cards can then be attached to the station poster sign with tape.

Station 2. Pray for God's protection of your life.

Before the session, guide students to prepare stories from David's life for this station.

During the event, have the students tell about times when God protected David: fighting Goliath, being a fugitive with Saul trying to kill him. Instruct students to ask the participants to tell a time when God protected them. Then the students will have the participants hold hands and ask one person to pray for God's protection for the group.

Station 3. Repent of sin in your life.

Before the session, guide students to prepare stories from David's life for this station.

During the event, have students tell about David's sin with Bathsheba, his killing her husband, and his repentance. Instruct the students to give each participant an index card and a pen or pencil. They will have the participants write their sins on the index card. Some people may want an extra index card.

Materials
photocopies of cards from page 75, pens or pencils, tape

Materials
index cards, matches, a coffee can, pens or pencils

When the participants finish, they will light the index card with a match and drop it into an empty gallon coffee can. Students will ask the participants to praise and thank God that He forgives and forgets our sins.

Station 4. Pray Scripture to God.

Before the session, instruct the students to mark a Bible with bookmarks at several Scriptures that speak about trusting God. For example: Proverbs 3:5, 6; Psalm 25:4, 5; Isaiah 8:17. Instruct the students to write the Scriptures on an overhead transparency with various colors of overhead pens. Gather Bibles, overhead transparencies, overhead pens, and an overhead projector for this station.

Students will read the Scriptures they have chosen and ask the participants to add to the list. The students will add the Scriptures to their overhead transparency. The students will have the participants pick a Scripture to pray to God. They will go around the circle and take turns praying a sentence prayer.

Materials
Bibles, bookmarks, overhead transparency, pens, and projector

Station 5. Pray for each other.

Before the session, ask students to think of something they would like others to pray about. It could be their ability to build a trusting relationship, courage to trust God, strength to tell others about their relationship with God, or their understanding of a particular circumstance.

During the event, students will instruct the participants to write their prayer requests on an index card and add it to a basket. Then each participant will take an index card from the basket and pray silently for the person's request on the card. When he has prayed, the participant will sign his name on the back of the card.

When the event is over, the students will find their index cards in the basket. They will be encouraged to see all of the signatures of people who prayed for their requests on their cards.

Materials
pens or pencils, index cards, basket

Unit 3

Belief Blast-off

Preteens are changing intellectually. They are becoming more aware of the "big picture". They are no longer content with seeing the world in isolated bits and pieces. They desire to see how facts and ideas interrelate. They are becoming more systematic, more capable of integrating facts and ideas into a unified system.

A preteen who has been raised in the church has learned much about the way of the Lord by the time he reaches this age. For the most part that knowledge has been in isolated Bible stories and moral precepts. The preteen needs to be able to synthesize these parts into a unified whole. Although they will not use the term, they need to develop a theology.

The Bible is not silent about this need. In the book of Luke, we see the description of Mary sorting through the wonderful and confusing events surrounding Jesus' birth. *What does it all mean? How do angel visits, shepherd's vigils, and prophetic visions fit into a unified whole?* Twice Luke states that Mary "treasured these things in her heart" (2:19, 51). Understanding the "heart" to be the seat of cognitive function, not the emotions, Luke is saying that Mary, with God's help, pieced together the events in the life of the infant and boy Jesus with her other experiences with God to come to a complete understanding of who Jesus was.

This is not dissimilar to the Psalmist's description of a mature

Unit Objective: Students will clarify their belief system, discover how it should influence their actions, and find ways to take positive Christian action.

Session 1
Scripture: Acts 17:24-31
Know that the God of the Bible is all-powerful, separate from man yet present with him, moral, and loving.
Feel reverence for such a mighty, compassionate God.
Compare God's characteristics to their own.

Session 2
Scripture: Genesis 1:26; Romans 7:14-25
Know that man, while created to be like God, has been broken by sin, making him incapable of doing good on his own.
Feel despair at the hopeless state of man without God.
Seek a solution to this problem.

Session 3
Scripture: Romans 8:1-17
Know that Jesus both pays for man's sins and gives him a new nature with which he can please God.
Feel the joy of being reunited with God.
Plan to share Jesus with others.

Session 4
Scripture: Ephesians 4:1-13; Romans 12:1, 2; 1 Corinthians 12:27—13:13
Know the big issues that separate Catholics and Protestants (What is the church's role in delivering God's grace

man or woman of God. Such a person "hides God's word in the heart" (Psalm 119:11). This process of synthesizing facts and ideas about God into a systematic view of the world results in godly living. Therefore it is the goal of this unit to begin that same process in your preteens. These sessions will help students clarify their belief systems, piecing once isolated facts about God and morality together, helping them catch a glimpse of the "big picture" of Christian living.

Session 1 begins this venture. What do Christians mean when they speak of this Being known as God? How do all of those stories about His actions build a complete picture of the Deity? Students will begin to understand that an all-powerful, all-knowing, creating, loving, and good Father of life, by His very existence, overshadows even our greatest attributes. Christian theology begins with an awe of Jehovah.

Session 2 takes an honest look at human beings. While they have heard the word "sin" many times and should be able to list many sinful acts, preteens need to begin to examine the implications of moral transgressions in light of a morally perfect God. How can man be both a noble creation of God and yet consistently perform acts of unspeakable evil? Students will begin to understand the devastating effects of sin on man and despair at the thought of separation from the Source of Truth and Life.

Session 3 completes the framework of basic Christian theology. A loving God desires to rescue man from the fruit of his transgressions. A just and good God must punish evil. Only by providing a Savior to pay the penalty for sin can God reunite man with Himself. Students will begin to understand that Jesus took our "death penalty" on Himself, and also gives us a new nature that is capable of obedience.

Session 4 addresses a question that may be raised after the first three sessions. "If basic Christianity is believing in an all-powerful, holy God, man who is separated from Him by sin, and a Savior whose job is to restore man to his intended state, why do different churches exist?" This session helps students understand some of the big issues that separate those who claim the name of Christ. Although this session will not answer all of the complex issues that separate believers, it will point to the ultimate answer. Christians must prayerfully study God's Word, seeking to conform to its dictates and practices.

The bonus sessions complement the content covered in the four classroom sessions. To **Bridge the Gap,** your students will join parents to honor those who consistently live the basics of their faith. In this service of testimony and praise, students will see that Christianity is more than ideas and principles, but a pathway for living on which others travel before them and with them.

to man?), Evangelicals and Liberals (How do changing times influence the message of the church?), and Charismatics and Non-charismatics (How does the Spirit equip Christians for service?).

Feel the urgency of modeling church doctrines and practices to the church of the New Testament.

Compare the doctrines and practices of their congregation to the Bible.

Family Session Idea
Faith Fleet Academy (A service of praise and personal testimony by adults of how their faith has changed their lives)

Service Project Idea
Creating the Captain's Log (Researching the history of their denomination and congregation)

Your preteens will **Go to Extremes** by researching the history of your particular congregation and denomination. They will create a historical document that will encourage others in your church.

Music Resources

Music is a tremendous tool for introducing ideas, communicating content, or reinforcing that which has been taught. Here are a few suggested songs from popular contemporary Christian artists. You may wish to try listening to and discussing one of these lesson-related tunes as an alternative closing activity or to review a preceding session.

Session	Song	Artist	CD
1 (God)	"Never Gonna Be as Big as Jesus"	Audio Adrenaline	*Bloom*, Forefront, 1996
	"God"	Rebecca St. James	*God*, Forefront, 1996
2 (Man)	"Never Cease to Amaze Me"	Three Crosses	*Three Crosses*, Benson, 1995
	"In the Light"	dc Talk	*Jesus Freak*, Forefront, 1996
3 (Jesus)	"The Champion"	Carman	*The Champion*, Myrrh, 1986
	"Free"	Steven Curtis Chapman	*Signs of Life*, Sparrow, 1996
4 (Church)	"Common Creed"	Wes King	*Common Creed*, Reunion, 1995

Daily Devotions

God has given us His Word so that we can know more about Him and ourselves. Read the verses listed each day. By studying the Bible, you will learn more of the wonderful adventure God has for you.

Day	Week 1 Majesty of God	Week 2 Nature of Man	Week 3 Mission of Jesus	Week 4 Design of the Church
Monday	God Is Creator Genesis 1:1—2:3	Man Is Special Psalm 8:3-8	A Mighty Savior Isaiah 9:6, 7	Unity Psalm 133
Tuesday	God Gives Law Exodus 20:1-17	Man Sinned Genesis 3	A Suffering Savior Isaiah 53	Power Matthew 16:18, 19
Wednesday	God Is Timeless Psalm 90:1-4	Man Is Mortal Psalm 90:5-10	A Humble Savior Philippians 2:5-11	Love John 13:34, 35
Thursday	God Is Mighty 2 Samuel 22:32-35	Man Needs God Isaiah 55:1, 2	A Risen Savior Matthew 28:1-10	Purity 2 Corinthians 6:14-18
Friday	God Is Love 1 John 4:7-18	Man Is Sinful Romans 3:10-18	A Returning Savior 1 Thessalonians 4:13-18	Encouragement Hebrews 10:19-25

Session 1

God— In Charge at Mission Control

Scripture: Acts 17:24-31

Know that the God of the Bible is all-powerful, separate from man yet present with him, moral, and loving.
Feel reverence for such a mighty, compassionate God.
Compare God's characteristics to their own.

Get Into the Game

Before class, find, purchase, or borrow two large inflatable beach toys. If you do not have the original containers for them, find a small bag or box for each in which the completely deflated toy will fit snugly. For the purpose of this game, the larger the inflatable toy, the better. We recommend an air mattress or inner tube.

Divide your class into two groups. Give each group an inflated beach toy and its container. On your signal, groups are to deflate their toy completely and place it completely into its container. Remind your team that to win they must neither damage the toy nor the container.

After the contest is over and a winning team has been declared, ask them why the activity was difficult. Agree that it is difficult to take something that is so large and force it down to size.

Introduce the session by saying that our relationship with God is very similar to this game in one way. God is so much larger than any of the "containers" in which we like to put Him. Ask students to think of different ways people like to describe God. For example, they may think of God as a "spy in the sky" constantly observing us, as a kindly grandparent we come to visit once a week, or as an ill-tempered guard keeping us from having any fun. Explain that a correct view of God is the beginning point of Christian belief. Students will discover that God is bigger than any of these previously mentioned ideas.

Materials
two large inflatable beach toys and their containers

Step 1

Activity #1

Have this group choose a captain. Give the captain the two colors of highlighters. This group will gather around the large manuscript you have made of today's Scripture text and analyze it. They will have their captain use one color to highlight every part of the text that describes what God is like, or what He does or has done. They will have their captain use the other color to highlight those portions of the text that describe what God is not like or what He doesn't do.

As students work, help them understand and analyze the text as necessary. Some suggested responses include:

What God is like—

made the earth, made everything in the earth, master of heaven and earth (v. 24)

gives men life, gives men everything (v. 25)

made first man, made every nation on earth, determined history of nations, determined boundaries of nations (v. 26)

wants men to look for Him, wants men to reach out to Him for help, wants men to find Him (v. 27)

is all around us, is our father (v. 28)

overlooked man's ignorance in the past, now commands people to repent (v. 30)

set a day for judgment, selected Jesus to be that judge, raised Jesus from the dead (v. 31).

What God is not like—

is not contained in temples built by people (v. 24)

does not need people to take care of Him (v. 25)

is not far from any of us (v. 27)

not like a statue or idol made of even the finest materials (v. 29).

Materials
large piece of newsprint or poster board with the words of Acts 17:24-31 written on it in manuscript form, two colors of highlighters

Activity #2

Help students list some characteristics of God on the chalkboard. These may include: holiness, majesty, power, ability to create, care for His creatures, love, Father of Mankind, judge of sinful world, giver of guidance, faithfulness, wisdom, etc.

Ask students to work in pairs to find familiar hymns or choruses that describe one or more of those characteristics. Help them as they begin their search. Make sure that they can explain what characteristic(s) of God are listed in the song and that they know the song well enough to sing it. Some songs and characteristics include:

Creator—This Is My Father's World

Protector and Provider—He's Got the Whole World in His Hands

Materials
hymnals and chorus books

Love—For God So Loved the World
Holiness—Holy, Holy, Holy
Mercy—I Will Sing of the Mercies of the Lord
Power—Great is the Lord, O Worship the King

To conclude this assignment, make a list of five to ten songs. Review the attributes of God each song describes and review the tune to each song in preparation for Step 2.

Activity #3

Brainstorm with this group, helping them list characteristics of God. See the preceding two activities for suggested responses.

Mount the large piece of newsprint on the wall. Give students access to markers. Explain that they will begin to draw a portrait of God on this paper. Each will think of one or more of the characteristics of God that they have just listed and will attempt to illustrate them in some way. Each student may draw anywhere on the paper. The goal of the group is to completely fill the paper with drawings that describe God.

As students work, help them with ideas as necessary. They may illustrate God's power with lightning bolts or God's love with hearts. They may wish to show God's guidance with road signs pointing the way to Him or God's creativity by illustrating the variety of creatures He has made. An eye or an outstretched hand may illustrate God's presence and provision.

Materials
large sheet of newsprint, markers

Step 2

Group 2 will begin this section of the session by leading the other two groups in a game of "Name That Tune." Ask Groups 1 and 3 each to select a captain. Flip a coin to determine which team begins. That first team will challenge, "I can name that tune in (a certain number) notes." The second team may answer with a smaller number. The first team may choose to respond with a lower number. Continue until one team has the lowest unchallenged bid. Then Group 2 will select one of the songs they found in Step 1 and will hum the number of notes that the beginning team bid. If that first team cannot identify the song, the other team will get to hear an additional note of the song hummed. Play continues until the song is identified. When the song is identified, Group 2 will explain the characteristics of God they found in that song.

Play continues in this manner for several rounds. Declare the team that identified the most songs to be the winner. Review the list of the attributes of God described in the songs.

Then allow Group 3 to explain their artwork. Allow each artist to explain the symbolism used in their work to describe God.

Conclude with Group 1 reviewing its study of Acts 17:24-31. They will be able to point out what the Bible says about who God is and what He does. Help the class understand the various parts of God's nature and how the Bible's description of God is so much greater than many popular ideas of God discussed earlier.

Step 3

Gather the entire class into a large circle for this response activity. Begin with the person to your left. That person will finish the following sentence:

A person who I think is really great is . . .

The next person to the left will respond by completing this statement:

This person is considered great because . . .

The next person to the left will finish this statement:

If I were to meet this person I would feel . . .

Finally, the next person to the left will conclude by completing:

Compared to what I just learned about God, this person . . .

For example, the first student may select a famous athlete. The second person will conclude that the athlete is known for his strength. The third student may feel intimidated by being around someone so large and strong. The fourth student may conclude that as strong as that athlete is, he is not nearly as strong as God.

Continue this activity until several celebrities are named and compared to God's greater attributes. Then conclude by asking, "If we feel this way in the presence of these people, how should we feel if we truly stood in the presence of God who is much greater?"

Take It to the Next Level

To conclude this session, students will compare God's characteristics to their own best characteristics. Give each student a photocopy of page 99. As they work on this page individually, walk among them to help them as necessary. They will list something that they do of which they are proud. They will then identify the characteristic that such an action exemplifies. For example, a student may be proud of her ability to earn good grades in math. That indicates intelligence. They will then list how God shows that characteristic. In this example they may write that God can count all of the stars in the universe and knows the number of grains of sand on the beach. They will then compare God's greatness to their own.

Materials
photocopies of page 99, pencils or pens

97   God—In Charge

Allow volunteers to share their responses. Conclude with the following litany. They will respond to each of your statements with, "Great are You, Lord. We praise You!"

Leader: Our God, we have studied about your characteristics today.

Response: Great are You, Lord. We praise You!

Leader: You are our Creator. There is nothing that is not made by You.

Response: Great are You, Lord. We praise You!

Leader: You are not like us. You are greater than us and beyond our description.

Response: Great are You, Lord. We praise You!

Leader: But at the same time, You choose to be all around us.

Response: Great are You, Lord. We praise You!

Leader: Your goodness is beyond any goodness that we have.

Response: Great are You, Lord. We praise You!

Leader: Yet You love us and want us to love You.

Response: Great are You, Lord. We praise You!

Leader: In Jesus' name, Amen.

Family Resemblance

Something I do very well is…

_____
_____
_____
_____
_____
_____

The characteristic that this action reveals in me is…

_____
_____
_____
_____
_____
_____
_____
_____

God has that characteristic too. I see it because God…

_____
_____
_____
_____
_____
_____
_____

God, compared to you, my ability…

_____
_____
_____
_____
_____

Session 2
Man— Lost in Space

Scripture: Genesis 1:26; Romans 7:14-25

Know that man, while created to be like God, has been broken by sin, making him incapable of doing good on his own.
Feel despair at the hopeless state of man without God.
Seek a solution to the problem.

Get Into the Game

Before class, set up an obstacle course consisting of four to five chairs spaced about three feet apart. The chairs do not need to be in a straight line. Also remove the bathroom tissue from its wrapping and insert a broom handle into each roll.

Divide your class into two groups. Give each group a broom handle with a roll of tissue. Have each group choose one space walker and two pilots.

Allow one group at a time to navigate the obstacle course. They will begin by standing about three feet from the first chair. The space walker will place one end of the tissue in his shoe, making sure that it is secure. The pilots will sit on the floor a few feet apart, each holding an end of the broom handle with the tissue roll between them. On your signal the space walker will begin moving through the course, trailing the tissue behind him. He will weave between the chairs, passing to the right of the first, the left of the second, the right of the third, and so forth. The pilots will hold the broom handle and make sure the roll spins freely, allowing an unbroken line of tissue to follow the space walker. The space walker will weave through the course and return to the pilots. Then he will retrace his course as the pilots carefully roll the tissue back on to the roll. If the tissue breaks at any time during the space walk, the walker must go to the break nearest the beginning of the course, place the broken end of tissue in his shoe, and continue the course from that spot. The space walk is complete when the walker returns and an unbroken lifeline of tissue the length of the course has been rewound onto the roll. The teams will be competing for the shortest time to run the course.

After the contest is over and a winning team has been

Materials
three rolls of bathroom tissue and two broom handles, a watch with a second hand, chairs

declared, hold up the winning team's roll of tissue and the remaining, unused roll of tissue. The difference in the two rolls should be obvious.

Introduce the lesson by saying that this game illustrates what the Bible says about mankind. We were made to be pure and clean, but after negotiating the obstacle course of life, even for a short time, we find ourselves far from our original and intended state. We are wrinkled, dirty, and torn.

Step 1

Activity #1

Prepare photocopies of page 105 for everyone in this group. In this activity, students will look at key verses from the lesson text and paraphrase each into more complex language. Have a thesaurus and/or a dictionary of synonyms and antonyms available to help students complete this task.

As students work, help them understand each verse and make accurate translations. Encourage them to have fun and experiment with unfamiliar words. Verses and sample answers follow:

"So God created man in his own image" (Genesis 1:27)—*Consequently, the Deity fabricated Homo Sapiens to bear semblance to Himself.*

"For all have sinned and fall short of the glory of God" (Romans 3:23)—*Thus, the whole of humanity has transgressed Divine statutes, thereby failing to attain celestial splendor.*

"I am unspiritual, sold as a slave to sin" (Romans 7:14)—*My nature remains corporeal, ransomed as a thrall of inequity.*

"When I want to do good, evil is right there with me" (Romans 7:21)—*In whatever season I long to perform beneficence, I am in immediate propinquity with the diabolical.*

"What a wretched man I am!" (Romans 7:24)—*My depravity is extraordinary!*

To conclude this group assignment, help students summarize what they have learned. Lead them into understanding that the Bible teaches that we have been created in God's image, but that image has been broken by sin. Our human nature rebels against our godly nature and thwarts its desire to do right.

Materials
photocopies of page 105, pencils, thesauruses, dictionaries of synonyms and antonyms

Activity #2

Lay the large piece of newsprint on the floor. Have a volunteer lie on the paper. Ask other students to trace the silhouette of the volunteer.

Divide the silhouette in half lengthwise with a straight line. Have students label the left side of the silhouette "Godly

Materials
large piece of newsprint, markers, Bibles

Nature" and the right side "Human Nature." Read the following Scriptures aloud: Genesis 1:27; Romans 3:10; 23; 7:14-25. After each verse is read, ask if students heard a description of people that fits into one of the two halves of the silhouette. Allow a volunteer to write any description in the appropriate half of the drawing.

Some suggested phrases and their placement on the silhouette follow:

Godly Nature

"So God created man in his own image..." (Genesis 1:27); "for I have the desire to do what is good..." (Romans 7:18); "the good I want to do..." (Romans 7:19); "I want to do good..." (Romans 7:21); "For in my inner being I delight in God's law" (Romans 7:22); "I myself in my mind am a slave to God's law..." (Romans 7:25)

Human Nature

"There is no one righteous, not even one" (Romans 3:10); "for all have sinned and fall short of the glory of God..." (Romans 3:23); "I am unspiritual, sold as a slave to sin" (Romans 7:14); "I do not understand what I do" (Romans 7:15); "For what I want to do I do not do..." (Romans 7:15); "what I hate I do" (Romans 7:15); "sin living in me" (Romans 7:17, 20); "nothing good lives... my sinful nature" (Romans 7:18); "the evil I do not want to do—this I keep on doing" (Romans 7:19); "evil is right there with me" (Romans 7:21); "a prisoner of the law of sin..." (Romans 7:23); "What a wretched man I am!" (Romans 7:24); "body of death..." (Romans 7:24); "a slave to the law of sin" (Romans 7:25).

To conclude this group assignment, help students summarize what they have learned. Lead them into understanding that the Bible teaches that we have been created in God's image, but that image has been broken by sin. Our human nature rebels against our godly nature and thwarts its desire to do right.

Allow students to add appropriate decorations and designs to the silhouettes in any time remaining.

Activity #3

Write the following names and Scripture references on the board:

Noah—Genesis 6:8, 9; 9:1, 20, 21
Samson—Judges 13:2-5, 24; 16:17-20
David—Acts 13:22; 2 Samuel 7:8, 9; 2 Samuel 11
Peter—Matthew 16:13-19; Acts 5:12-16; Galatians 2:11-13

Work with preteens to create a skit. They will be in a meeting of the Fraternal Association of Men of Excellence (FAME). Their job is to pick out the most perfect man who ever lived.

Materials
Bibles

They will suggest each of the names listed and give reasons for their choices. In each case, however, another member will object, pointing out a serious fault in each of these men. The Scripture references contain the information they need. For example, Noah was seen as a righteous man in a sinful world, but after the ark landed, he made wine and became drunk.

To conclude this group assignment, help students summarize what they have learned. Even the best men who ever lived committed sins.

Step 2

Begin by writing the following Scripture references on the board: Genesis 1:27; Romans 3:23; Romans 7:14; Romans 7:21; Romans 7:24.

Ask volunteers from Group 1 to select and read one of their paraphrased verses from their activity. Allow members of Groups 2 and 3 to match the paraphrase with the references you have written on the board.

After playing several rounds, ask Group 2 to display and explain their silhouette. Summarize these first two group presentations by noting that mankind suffers a horrible division. We recognize that goodness exists, but we are incapable of being good with our own strength alone.

Introduce Group 3's skit by noting that we see that truth illustrated in even the greatest of Bible heroes. Allow Group 3 to close this section of the session with their performance.

Materials
chalk and chalkboard

Step 3

Keep the class in the three groups from the preceding two steps. Ask students to imagine that they are space aliens sent to gather evidence about life on earth. They have already read what the Bible says about people. They are going to gather information to see if it is true that man has difficulty doing right.

Give each group a newspaper and a highlighter. Assign Group 1 to skim the national and international news, Group 2, the local news, and Group 3, advertising and entertainment sections of the paper. They should highlight any evidence of man's sinful nature they find.

After a few minutes, allow your surveillance teams to report. Conclude that it is easy to see that the biblical view of man, separated from God, is correct.

Materials
newspapers, highlighters

Take It to the Next Level

A white flag is universally recognized as a signal of surrender. Conclude this session by deciding that the only reasonable response that fallen man has to an awesome God is unconditional surrender.

Give each student a piece of white cloth and a dowel rod. Give everyone access to glue and fabric markers. Students should write the verse reference, Romans 7:24, on their flags and staple them to the flagpoles.

Ask students to take their white flags home and display them in their rooms as a reminder of their need to surrender to God daily.

Conclude with a prayer recognizing God's greatness and our great need for Him.

Materials
12" lengths of small dowel rods, 3" x 5" strips of white cloth, fabric paint or markers, stapler

Verbal Overload

Sometimes we can understand something better when we put it into different words. In this case use a thesaurus or dictionary of synonyms to make these verses from the Bible harder to understand. The first one is done for you as an example.

"So God created man in his own image" (Genesis 1:27).
Consequently, the Deity fabricated Homo Sapiens to bear semblance to Himself.

"For all have sinned and fall short of the glory of God" (Romans 3:23).
_____
_____
_____
_____

"I am unspiritual, sold as a slave to sin" (Romans 7:14).
_____
_____
_____
_____

"When I want to do good, evil is right there with me" (Romans 7:21).
_____
_____
_____
_____

"What a wretched man I am!" (Romans 7:24).
_____
_____
_____
_____

Session 3

Jesus—Sent on the Universe's Greatest Rescue Mission

Scripture: Romans 8:1-17

Know that Jesus both pays for man's sins and gives him a new nature with which he can please God.
Feel the need to respond to the love of God.
Plan to deepen their relationship with God.

Get Into the Game

Before class, draw six to seven small (1" diameter) circles in random locations on one of the drop cloths. Use a pen or pencil to make a hole in the center of each circle. You will also need to arrange for an appropriate space in which to perform this activity. You'll need approximately an 8' x 8' open space with a floor protected from water spills.

Divide your class into two groups. One group at a time will perform Round 1 of the Water Rescue Mission. The group will hold up the non-punctured drop cloth between them, with half of the group supporting one side and half supporting the other. Give an empty cup to a person at one corner of the cloth and a full cup of water to a person at the opposite corner. The job of each group is to guide spilled water across the drop cloth into the empty cup with the smallest amount of water lost. Use the graduated measuring cup to measure the amount of water rescued. The group that rescues the most water wins that round.

Play the second round in the same way, only using the marked and punctured drop cloth. The rescue is more difficult because the water must be directed around the holes. If it is appropriate in your setting, you may choose to play a third round. In this round the punctured cloth is used, but a member of the group is under the cloth helping direct the water and risking getting wet.

After the contest is over, introduce the lesson. "As we have studied last session, man is like the water, lost in a world full of dangers. We cannot save ourselves; we need someone to make the effort and to take the risks in rescuing us."

Materials

two inexpensive plastic drop cloths, two cups of equal size, graduated measuring cup, cardboard circle 1" in diameter, pen or pencil

Step 1

Before dividing the class into groups, write the following outline of Romans 8:1-17 on the board:
- vv. 1-4—Jesus rescues sinful man.
- vv. 5-11—Jesus restores sinful man.
- vv. 12-17—Jesus rewards man.

Activity #1

Ask students to imagine that Romans 8:1-17 was to be released as a book. Their job is to think of a title for it and to design the front and back covers. They will want to pick out certain images from these verses and illustrate them.

As students work, help them understand the main points of the passage and to get ideas for illustrations. For example, the idea of being "set . . . free from the law of sin and death" could be illustrated with broken chains. A dove inside of a silhouette of a person's head may picture "the mind controlled by the Spirit." Point out the rich images in this passage such as "sending his own Son . . . to be a sin offering", "your body is dead because of sin", an "heirs of God and co-heirs with Christ". Encourage them to be imaginative in their illustrations.

To conclude this group assignment, help students summarize what they have learned. Lead them into understanding that the Bible teaches that Jesus took the death sentence we deserved as sinners, thereby paying for our crimes against God. He then gave us the Holy Spirit to empower us to do right and avoid further enslavement to sin. Finally, He makes us God's sons who will inherit all of the goodness of the heavenly kingdom.

Materials
two sheets of poster board, markers, Bibles

Activity #2

Haiku (pronounced HI-koo) is a simple Japanese verse form. These three-line poems contain five syllables in lines one and three with seven syllables in line two. Writing haiku is a fun way of expressing an important idea succinctly.

Divide this group into three subgroups. Assign each subgroup one of the sections of the Scripture outlined on the board. They will read the passage and summarize its content as a haiku. Help them as much as necessary to distill the content into poetry. Some sample haiku follows:

We are all guilty.
God sent a sin offering.
No condemnation (vv. 1-4).

Sinful man is fired.
Holy Spirit takes control,
Restoring life, peace (vv. 5-11).

Materials
paper, pencils, Bibles

Jesus' Rescue Mission

We are slaves no more,
but adopted sons of God,
Heirs to all His wealth (vv. 12-17).

To conclude this group assignment, help students summarize what they have learned. Lead them to understand that the Bible teaches that Jesus took the death sentence we deserved as sinners, thereby paying for our crimes against God. He then gave us the Holy Spirit to empower us to do right and avoid further enslavement to sin. Finally, He makes us God's sons who will inherit all of the goodness of the heavenly kingdom.

Activity #3

Work with this group to create a skit. They will imagine that the apostle Paul was asked to appear on a book review program. The interviewer will ask him questions about the mission of Jesus that he wrote about in Romans 8. The group will select someone to play Paul and another to play the interviewer. The group will review this section of Scripture to come up with questions the reviewer may have and answers Paul would give. Some sample questions and answers would include:

Q: Paul, you say that people who are in a relationship with Jesus are no longer condemned by God for their sins (8:1). How can that be?

A: God sent His son to pay the penalty for man's sin. Man is guilty of breaking God's law. God offered Jesus as an payment for that guilt (8:3).

Q: Couldn't God just overlook sin as no "big deal?"

A: But sin is a "big deal." If God treats sin as something insignificant, He would no longer be righteous. A penalty for sin is required. Because God is loving as well as righteous, however, He paid the penalty (8:4).

Q: You seem to be saying in your book that even if man's sins are forgiven, he is unable to start over and stop sinning (8:7, 8). What about that?

A: That is true. Man is guilty because of sins he commits. But he commits sin because his fallen nature leads him in that direction. The second benefit of the work of Jesus is that He fixes our broken nature by giving us His Holy Spirit (8:9).

Q: What is this "Spirit of sonship" you write about (8:15)?

A: When people accept Jesus' payment for their sins and allow His Spirit to direct them away from sin, they become sons of God. Like sons growing up in a family, there will be discipline and instruction, but finally the son inherits everything the father has for him (8:17).

To conclude this group assignment, help students summarize what they have learned. Help them understand that the Bible teaches that Jesus took the death sentence we deserved

Materials
Bibles

as sinners, thereby paying for our crimes against God. He then gave us the Holy Spirit to empower us to do right and avoid further enslavement to sin. Finally, He makes us God's sons who will inherit all of the goodness of the heavenly kingdom.

Step 2

Begin by asking Group 1 to display and explain their cover illustrations. Follow this by allowing volunteers from Group 2 to read and explain their haiku. Conclude this section of the session with Group 3's skit.

Step 3

Distribute photocopies of the Criss-Cross puzzle from page 110. Students will place words from the word list into the grid. Then they will transfer the words in the order listed below the puzzle to form six responses Christians should make to a loving God. Those responses are as follows:

    Worship His Glory
    Pray Daily
    Read His Word
    Encourage Other Believers
    Tell Friends About Jesus
    Lead Godly Lives

After students have completed the puzzle, review the answers together. Spend some time discussing why such responses are logical for people who realize they have been rescued from sin by a loving God.

Materials
photocopies of the puzzle on page 110, pencils

Take It to the Next Level

Close this session by asking students to consider the six responses discovered in Step 3. Ask them to number the responses from 1-6. They will put a 1 by the response they need the most work in improving, 2 by their next weakest response, etc.

After students have done so, lead and close a time of silent prayer. During that silent prayer time, ask students to pray for God's help in strengthening their weaker responses to Him.

Criss-Cross

Fill in the blanks of this puzzle with the words below. Then transfer the words in the order given at the bottom of the puzzle to list six responses we should make to the love of God.

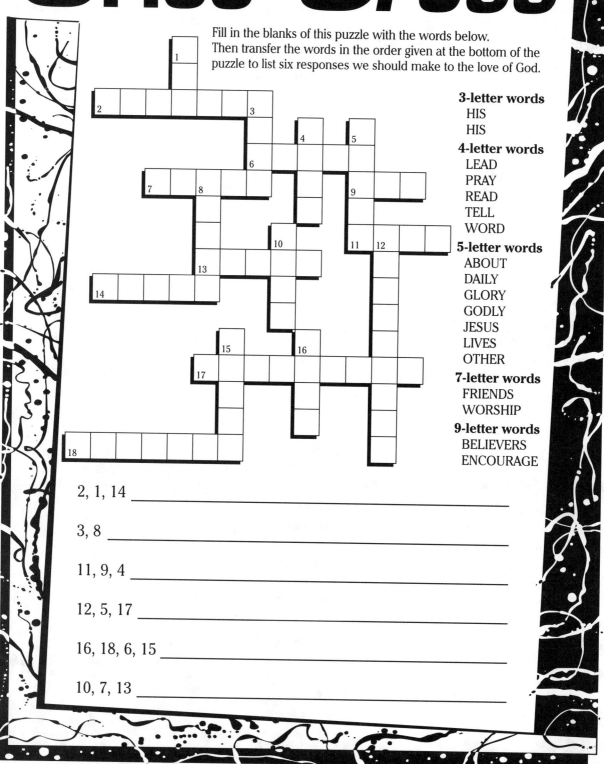

3-letter words
HIS
HIS

4-letter words
LEAD
PRAY
READ
TELL
WORD

5-letter words
ABOUT
DAILY
GLORY
GODLY
JESUS
LIVES
OTHER

7-letter words
FRIENDS
WORSHIP

9-letter words
BELIEVERS
ENCOURAGE

2, 1, 14 _____

3, 8 _____

11, 9, 4 _____

12, 5, 17 _____

16, 18, 6, 15 _____

10, 7, 13 _____

Session 4

Other Christians— Flying in Differing Spacecraft

Scripture: Ephesians 4:1-13; Romans 12:1, 2; 1 Corinthians 12:27—13:13

Know the big issues that separate Catholics and Protestants (What is the church's role in delivering God's grace to man?), Evangelicals and Liberals (How do changing times influence the message of the church?), and Charismatics and Non-charismatics (How does the Spirit equip Christians for service?).

Feel the urgency of modeling church doctrines and practices to the church of the New Testament.

Seek to learn how the doctrines and practices of their congregation compare to the Bible.

Materials
three large black plastic bags, three small parts from a bicycle

Get Into the Game

Before class, place a small part from a bicycle in each of the three plastic bags. The bicycle parts should be ones which are very different from each other and those that play a significant, but not central role in the operation of the bicycle. For example, a single spoke, a reflector, the cap from the inner tube, a spring from the seat, or a few links from the chain would all work well. *(Note: If you do not have access to a bicycle, use the parts from a telephone, blender, or any other small appliance that can be easily disassembled.)*

Divide your class into three groups. Give each group a bag, asking that they not look into it. Explain that they are explorers who have discovered a strange alien device. Their job is to reach into their bag and describe the alien device by using only their sense of touch.

Have each group prepare to answer the following questions:
1. Describe the shape of the alien device?
2. Of what material(s) is the device made?
3. What do you suppose is the use of the device?
4. What might be a good name for the device?

As groups work, make sure they use only their sense of touch. Help them answer the questions as necessary.

Allow each group to share the answers to their questions with the group. When all groups have answered the questions, allow groups to display what was in their bags. Explain that the alien device is a bicycle. Ask why no group correctly identified the device, its purpose, or was even able to give a clear description of it. Of course, the reason is that they spent their time concentrating only on a small part of the whole.

Introduce the lesson by comparing the divisions among

Christians to this activity. Could it be that we have so many churches because Christians often concentrate on a small part of God's plan rather than all of it?

Step 1

Before class, prepare each large sheet of newsprint or poster board by writing the following words on it with a marker:

Biblical Principle—

Controversy Surrounding that Principle—

Division #1's Name—

A Few Things Division #1 Believes About that Principle

Division #2's Name—

A Few Things Division #2 Believes About that Principle

Mount these sheets on the wall in different locations of the room. Divide the class into three groups, sending each group to a location by a mounted sheet of newsprint or poster board.

Materials
three large sheets of newsprint or poster board

Activity #1

Members of this group should read through the information on this study sheet. They will discuss this material, receiving necessary assistance from you. They will prepare answers for the questions written on the newsprint or poster board. After you are certain that their responses are complete and accurate, allow them to fill in their newsprint or poster board.

Their answers should be similar to these:

Biblical Principle—*Christians should try to keep unity in the church.*

Controversy Surrounding that Principle—*How do we keep the church unified?*

Division #1's Name—*Catholics*

A Few Things Division #1 Believes About that Principle

1. The church is unified under a human leader called the Pope.

2. God gives His gifts to men by their faith and through authorized actions of the church called sacraments.

3. God reveals truth both through the Scripture and through decisions and proclamations of the church throughout history.

Division #2's Name—*Protestants*

A Few Things Division #2 Believes About that Principle

1. The church is unified by Jesus alone and not by any human leader.

Materials
photocopies of Study Sheet 1 on page 116, marker

2. God's grace comes directly to man by faith, not through church ritual.

3. God reveals His truth through Scripture alone.

To conclude this group assignment, students should select a reporter who will summarize this information verbally to the rest of the class in Step 2.

Activity #2

Members of this group should read through the information on this study sheet. They will discuss this material receiving necessary assistance from you. They will prepare answers for the questions written on the newsprint or poster board. After you are certain that their responses are complete and accurate, allow them to fill in their newsprint or poster board.

Their answers should be similar to these:

Biblical Principle—*Christians must explain the basics of the gospel to others in ways that they will understand.*

Controversy Surrounding that Principle—*What are the basics of the gospel? Where do we find these basics?*

Division #1's Name—*Liberals*

A Few Things Division #1 Believes About that Principle

1. The church must teach the moral principles that will make the world a better place now.

2. The Bible is one place to look for these principles, but it is not always historically accurate.

3. Man's reasoning ability and emotions can lead him into God's truth.

Division #2's Name—*Conservatives*

A Few Things Division #2 Believes About that Principle

1. The church should teach man's responsibility to God first, then man's responsibility to each other will fall into place.

2. The Bible is historically reliable because it has been written and kept that way by God Himself.

3. Only Spirit-led Bible study will lead men to truth.

To conclude this group assignment, students should select a reporter who will summarize this information verbally to the rest of the class in Step 2.

Activity #3

Members of this group should read through the information on this study sheet. They will discuss this material receiving necessary assistance from you. They will prepare answers for the questions written on the newsprint or poster board. After you are certain that their responses are complete and accurate, allow them to fill in their newsprint or poster board.

Their answers should be similar to these:

Biblical Principle—*Christians are equipped to obey and serve*

Materials
photocopies of Study Sheet 2 on page 117, marker

Materials
photocopies of Study Sheet 3 on page 118, marker

God by the Holy Spirit.

Controversy Surrounding that Principle—*What gifts does the Holy Spirit give Christians today?*

Division #1's Name—*Charismatics*

A Few Things Division #1 Believes About that Principle

1. All of the gifts God gave believers in the early church are available to all Christians today.

2. God can and does give His people reliable prophetic messages today.

Division #2's Name—*Non-charismatics*

A Few Things Division #2 Believes About that Principle

1. Certain gifts given to the early church were for that time only, not for today.

2. The Bible is the only source of reliable messages from God today.

To conclude this group assignment, students should select a reporter who will summarize this information verbally to the rest of the class in Step 2.

Step 2

Allow each group to report on its findings. Remember that the issues surrounding these church divisions are complex and will inspire many questions from your students. Answer as many as you feel comfortable answering and as many as time allows. This session is only meant to be a brief introduction. Do not feel that you have to resolve every issue or answer every question completely during this time.

It is important, however, that your students conclude this section of the lesson understanding the basis for Christian unity. Stress that we may not know all of the answers right now, but we do have a reliable place to find answers. We must study the Scriptures if we are to be the church described in those pages.

Step 3

Write the following Scripture references on the board: John 17:17; 2 Timothy 2:15; 2 Timothy 3:16, 17; 1 Peter 2:2.

Allow students to work in groups of two or three for this activity. Ask each group to select one of these passages about the value of the Bible to the Christian and the church. They will then develop and illustrate an advertising slogan based upon that passage. For example, they could draw a large crowd of people and a few standing apart from the crowd holding a Bible. The slogan, "Truth sets us apart from the crowd!" would illustrate John 17:17. Carpenter tools and a house built out of a

Materials
Bibles, paper, pencils, markers

Bible could be entitled, "Build on this!" illustrating 2 Timothy 2:15. The slogan, "God's Milk—Today and Every Day!" underneath a picture of a person sporting a milk mustache and holding a Bible could illustrate 1 Peter 2:2.

Help students as they work. Conclude this activity by allowing each group to share their slogans and advertisements. State again that only by reading and following the Bible can we unify all believers into God's one church.

Take It to the Next Level

Distribute paper and pencils to every group from the preceding activity. Ask them to write any questions that they may have about the beliefs of their congregation. You will collect and use them for the **Go to Extremes** session.

Close this session with a time of silent prayer. During that silent prayer time, ask students to pray for God's help in strengthening their study and understanding of the Word.

Materials
paper, pencils

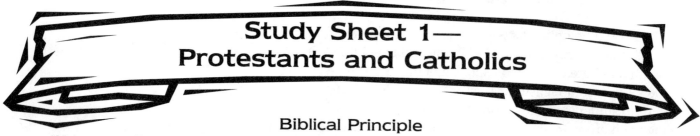

Study Sheet 1— Protestants and Catholics

Biblical Principle

"Make every effort to keep the unity of the Spirit through the bond of peace. There is one body and one Spirit—just as you were called to one hope when you were called—one Lord, one faith, one baptism; one God and Father of all, who is over all and through all and in all" (Ephesians 4:3-6).

Paul taught that there is only one church. This is logical because we have one message. That message is that a great and holy God saved sinful mankind by sacrificing His Son, Jesus. Therefore, we must make sure that the church remains one.

Controversy

It is logical that there is only one church. It is also logical to insist that Christians work to make sure that the church remains one. The controversy occurs when we ask, "How will this happen?" Should man strictly organize the church like a large corporation? Should there be an earthly head of the church who gives responsibility to some leaders, who then gives responsibility to lesser leaders, who regulate local groups of Christians? Or should Christians be led by God individually to begin a variety of congregations, not ruled by a world-wide organization, but by trust in God and obedience to the Bible alone?

Division—Catholics and Protestants

The word "catholic" means "universal" or "undivided." While many complex issues are a part of any religious group, we can safely say that three important principles are central to Catholicism. All of them have to do with the belief that there must be only one, undivided true church on earth.

1. The first principle is that the church is strictly organized under the ultimate human control of one person, the Bishop of Rome, commonly called the Pope. Catholics believe that God first placed Peter in charge of the church, and through the centuries placed that same authority in human hands. Under the pope are regional bishops, who supervise local priests.

2. The second principle is that God gives his gifts to men through faith and through the authorized actions of the church. These authorized actions are called "the sacraments." God binds a man and woman together through the sacrament of marriage. God forgives sins Christians commit after those sins are confessed to a priest and repentant response is taken in the sacrament of penance. God chooses those who would serve as priests by selecting them by the church—the sacrament of holy orders.

3. The third principle is that God reveals his truth by two streams. The first stream is through the Scriptures. The second stream is through the historical practices of the church.

Protestants received their name because they "protested" this strict organization of the church. They believe that God unifies His church, not a human leader. While there are many branches of Protestantism, we can say that they all oppose the three principles of Catholicism listed above.

1. Protestants do not believe that there is a human head of the church. Protestant congregations may be connected in some ways, but the strong link to one man believed to be a successor of the apostle Peter is not present.

2. Protestants believe that God's gifts come directly from God to man through faith. Every believer has direct access to God.

3. Protestants believe that God reveals His truth through Scripture alone. Church tradition may be in error. Only the Bible is always true.

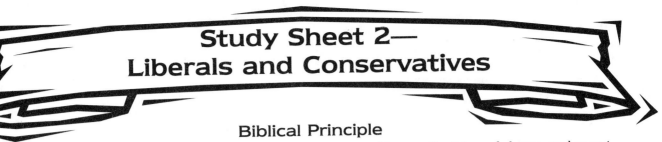

Study Sheet 2—Liberals and Conservatives

Biblical Principle

"What then is my reward? Just this: that in preaching the gospel I may offer it free of charge, and so not make use of my rights in preaching it. Though I am free and belong to no man, I make myself a slave to everyone, to win as many as possible. To the Jews I became like a Jew, to win the Jews. To those under the law I became like one under the law (though I myself am not under the law), so as to win those under the law. To those not having the law I became like one not having the law (though I am not free from God's law but am under Christ's law), so as to win those not having the law. To the weak I became weak, to win the weak. I have become all things to all men so that by all possible means I might save some" (1 Corinthians 9:18-22).

Paul taught that it is the believer's job to teach the gospel to others. Furthermore, we must teach **only** the gospel. We must put aside preferences we have learned from our culture.

Controversy

It is logical that we must teach only the gospel. It is also logical to insist that Christians not expect everyone to share the same opinions in order to be a Christian. The controversy occurs when we ask, "What are the basics of the gospel?" Should we look for basics in church traditions, in the Bible, or in man's own thoughts and feelings?

Division—Liberals and Conservatives

Liberal theology is found in what are usually called "mainline" Protestant denominations. There are many differences among theological liberals, but all would agree with some basic principles. All of these principles have to do with the belief that the message of the church must meet the needs of modern culture.

1. The first principle is that the church must teach man's responsibility to fellow man. By looking at the teachings of Jesus, the church must teach those principles of living that will bring peace and harmony to the brotherhood of Man. This emphasis has been called the "social gospel." The job of the church is to make the world a better place.

2. The second principle is that both church tradition and the Bible contain truth mixed with error. Relying upon either or both of these sources for truth is not enough. Generally it is believed that many of the stories in the Bible are myths that God used to teach true rules for living, but are not reliable history.

3. The third principle is that man can understand God's truth through his own reasoning ability and his feelings. We can learn much about God by studying His world logically and scientifically. We must also listen to our strong emotional longings for Someone we cannot understand through reason alone.

Conservative theology is found in what are often called "fundamentalist" and "evangelical" churches. Many differences exist among theological conservatives, but all would agree with some basic principles. All of these principles have to do with the belief that the message of the church must be true to the unchanging fundamentals of Christianity found in the Bible.

1. Conservatives believe that the church must teach man's responsibility to God. Man must be born again spiritually in order to please God. The brotherhood of man is important, but it will only be accomplished when man is in tune with God the Father.

2. Conservatives believe that the Bible is historically accurate and true in every way. The Bible is God's Word to man and must be obeyed.

3. Conservatives believe that man's reasoning and emotions are unreliable because they are stained by sin. Only by studying the Word of God, aided by the Holy Spirit, will man find truth.

Study Sheet 3—
Charismatics and Non-charismatics

Biblical Principle

"There are different kinds of gifts, but the same Spirit. There are different kinds of service, but the same Lord. There are different kinds of working, but the same God works all of them in all men. Now to each one the manifestation of the Spirit is given for the common good. To one there is given through the Spirit the message of wisdom, to another the message of knowledge by the means of the same Spirit, to another faith by the same Spirit, to another gifts of healing by that one Spirit, to another miraculous powers, to another prophecy, to another distinguishing between spirits, to another the ability to speak in different kinds of tongues, and to still another the interpretation of tongues" (1 Corinthians 12:4-10).

Paul taught that Christians are given the ability to serve God by the Holy Spirit. This agrees with the teaching that man is sinful and cannot please God with his own strength.

Controversy

Christians agree that the Holy Spirit equips believers to serve God. The controversy occurs when we ask, "What gifts does the Holy Spirit give Christians today?"

Division—Charismatics and Non-charismatics

The word "charismatic" comes from the Greek word meaning "free gifts." Not all charismatics believe exactly alike, but generally they will agree that the Holy Spirit desires to give Christians today the same free gifts of power and revelation as He gave to the early church.

1. Charismatics believe that the gifts listed above in 1 Corinthians 12 are still available to Christians today. These included speaking in a language that one has never learned (often called "speaking in tongues"), the power to heal supernaturally, and receiving direct messages from God (prophecy).

2. Charismatics believe that the Scriptures are God-inspired and are one's primary source of God's revelation to man. They further believe that God can and does give reliable prophetic messages to His people today as well.

Non-charismatics also believe that the Holy Spirit equips Christians for service with special gifts. Non-charismatics believe, however, that not all gifts given to the early church are meant to be active in the church today.

1. Non-charismatics generally believe that certain gifts (speaking in tongues, healing, prophecy) were given by God to convince people in the days of the early church that the message spoken by the apostles and early Christians was true. In those days the New Testament was being written and was not complete. Now that the New Testament is complete, they believe that "sign" gifts are no longer necessary. The truth of the Bible can speak for itself, not needing to be proven with miraculous signs.

2. Non-charismatics believe that the Scriptures are God-inspired and are the only source of God's special revelation to man. They distrust claims of special revelation today.

Bridge the Gap

Faith Fleet Academy

The main sessions of this unit have been extremely "theoretical." The fact is, Christianity has core beliefs that do need to be taught as you have. Nevertheless, our faith is extremely practical. The "theory" works! Those who live according to the principles you have taught can testify to God's reality and grace.

Your class will plan and lead a worship service of praise that features testimony from members of your congregation. You may choose to have this service during your regular meeting time. As an alternative, you may arrange with church leadership to have your youth lead a regularly scheduled worship time. Either way, it is important that parents and preteens plan, participate in, and attend such a time together.

Testimonies

You will need to recruit four speakers to prepare five-to-seven minute testimonies. It is recommended that you use parents, grandparents, or other members of your preteens' families as much as possible. The descriptions of the testimonies follow:

Testimony 1—He Has Been Faithful All of My Life

Select an older member of your congregation for this testimony. A grandparent of a student would be ideal. You need someone who has been a Christian for most of his or her life.

Have the person speak about his or her earliest memories of worshiping God and continued dedication to Him today.

Testimony 2—He Changed My Life

Do you know of anyone whom Jesus has changed dramatically? This is the person for this testimony. How was life before meeting Jesus? What changes have occurred since?

Testimony 3—He Led Me Through Hardship

Every congregation has a member who has faced and overcome tremendous obstacles through his faith. Ask such a person to describe his struggle and the difference Jesus made.

Testimony 4—He Empowers Me to Serve Him

It is not too early to encourage your preteens to consider vocational ministry. A member of your church staff could do that with this testimony. Ask this person to share reasons he has chosen to be a minister, and how God has blessed this decision.

Worship Leaders

A variety of roles for students and parents need to be filled in this service. If possible, use a student or parent as an accompanist. Secure student volunteers to lead the two prayers, lead songs, and read Scripture.

Bulletins

The reproducible bulletins are found on the next two pages. Type in names of speakers, song leaders, and others participating in the service before copying them. Type in a small biography of each speaker in the appropriate place inside the bulletin. You may wish to have all of your students sign the greetings on the back of the bulletin for another personal touch.

Your preteens may choose to color these bulletins if that is feasible for the size of your projected attendance. Students will need to fold bulletins and distribute them before the service begins.

Faith Fleet Academy
Learning from those who have gone boldly with God

Why Faith Fleet Academy?

We have studied the basics of our faith. While we learn much from classes, this is not enough. We need examples of older Christians whose lives teach us by example.

As we begin to explore God's great universe, the four people who are giving their testimonies in this service have served as an "advance team." They have gone before us, showing that we can also venture into unknown territories because our faithful God is there.

For that reason we honor these Christian role models as members of our Faith Fleet Academy!

Faith Fleet Academy

Learning from those who have gone boldly with God

Prayer

Welcome

The Greatness of God
Hymn—O Worship the King
Chorus—How Majestic Is Your Name
Scripture Reading—Psalm 8:1, 2
Testimony 1—He Has Been Faithful All My Life

The Need of Man
Hymn—Just As I Am
Scripture Reading—Psalm 51:1, 2
Testimony 2—He Changed My Life

The Work of Christ
Chorus—Lord, I Lift Your Name on High
Scripture Reading—1 Timothy 3:16
Testimony 3—He Led Me Through Hardship

The Victorious Church
Hymn—The Church's One Foundation
Chorus—We Are One In the Spirit
Scripture Reading—1 Peter 2:4, 5
Testimony 4—He Empowers Me to Serve Him

Closing Hymn—Faith Is the Victory

Closing Prayer

Our Speakers:

Go to Extremes

Creating the Captain's Log

The truths learned in the four main sessions have been alive for years in the Body of Christ, His Church. Preteens, however, live in a world of instant changes and short-lived fads. They need to be taught about that which endures and thrives through the ages. They need to become connected with the history of the church.

Great explorers kept log books. They recorded significant events in their adventures. This supplementary activity will aid your students in creating the "Captain's Log" for your congregation.

Secure a new scrapbook or photo album. You may wish to assign a student artist or two to create a cover for your log. When your log is complete, see that it becomes a part of your church library.

Assign students or groups of students to complete the following sections of the log:

Interviews—Two reproducible sheets on pages 125 and 126 will help students interview long-time members of your congregation and members of the ministerial staff. Look for a staff member or other church leader who could provide information on past ministers.

Reports—Two reproducible sheets on pages 127 and 128 will help students create a brief history of your congregation and a brief history of your denomination. You will need to make references available for this research. Check with your church office for any written information on your congregation's history. You will need to visit your church library and/or a public library for information concerning denominational history.

Student Questions—Compile the list of questions about your congregation and denomination written by your students in the Take It to the Next Level section of **Session 4.** Have students interview a knowledgeable church leader and write responses to each question.

Artifacts—Help students find copies of old bulletins, church newsletters, tracts, photos, and other artifacts for this book. Some extra copies of these items may be available in the files of the church office. Members of your congregation may have such items they would be willing to donate for this project.

Member Memories

What is your name? _____

When did you start attending this church? _____
_____
_____
_____

Why did you choose this church? _____
_____
_____
_____

What are your earliest memories of this church? _____
_____
_____
_____

What is your favorite memory of this church? _____
_____
_____
_____

What was the most difficult or exciting challenge that this church has met since you have been here? _____
_____
_____
_____

Minister Profile

Minister's name _____

Years of ministry at this church _____
_____
_____
_____
_____

Other important background and experience _____
_____
_____
_____
_____

Important accomplishments of the church during this ministry _____
_____
_____
_____
_____

Minister's dreams and goals for this church _____
_____
_____
_____
_____
_____

History of this Congregation

When was this congregation started? _____
_____

Why was this congregation started? _____
_____
_____

Who was the founding minister? _____
_____

List the names of charter members _____
_____
_____
_____
_____

Where has this congregation met over the years?
Describe any building programs. _____
_____
_____
_____
_____

List accomplishments of this congregation
(i.e. other churches started, missionaries sent and supported, etc.)
_____
_____
_____
_____
_____

History of our Denomination

Name of denomination _____

Important historical figures in the denomination _____
_____
_____
_____
_____

Important historical events of the denomination _____
_____
_____
_____
_____

Important beliefs of the denomination _____
_____
_____
_____
_____

Some books or articles to read to learn more about
our denomination _____
_____
_____
_____
_____